SUN COUNTRY
S T Y L E S

SUN COUNTRY STYLES

Published by Home Planners, LLC
Wholly owned by Hanley-Wood, LLC
Editorial and Corporate Offices:
3275 W. Ina Road, Suite 110
Tucson, Arizona 85741
Distribution Center:
29333 Lorie Lane
Wixom, Michigan 48393

President: Jayne Fenton
Executive Editor: Linda B. Bellamy
Managing Editor: Vicki Frank
Associate Editor: Kristin Schneidler
Plans Associate: Morenci Wodraska
Plans Assistant: Marian Haggard
Graphic Designer: Peter Zullo
Senior Production Manager: Sara Lisa
Production Manager: Brenda McClary

Front cover: Design HPT890001; see page 4 for floor
plans and details. Photograph ©Russell
Kingman/HDS.
Page 3: Design HPT890025; see page 31 for floor
plans and details. Photograph courtesy of Islands of
Beaufort, Beaufort, SC.
Back cover: Design HPT890002, see page 6 for floor
plans and details. Photograph by Bob Greenspan.

Printed in the United States of America
Library of Congress Catalog Card Number:
2002112987
ISBN softcover: 1-931131-14-7

TABLE OF CONTENTS

DESIGN
HPT890001

SQUARE FOOTAGE: 3,424
BONUS SPACE: 507 SQ. FT.
WIDTH: 82'-4" DEPTH: 83'-8"

THIS LOVELY FIVE-BEDROOM HOME exudes the beauty and warmth of a Mediterranean villa. The foyer views explode in all directions, with the dominant use of octagonal shapes throughout. Double doors lead to the master wing, which abounds with niches and ceiling detailing. The sitting area of the master bedroom has a commanding view of the rear gardens, and the master bath enjoys a dual-space design with a dressing area. A private bedroom suite just off the master suite is perfect for a guest room or home office. The formal living and dining rooms share expansive glass walls and marble or tile pathways. An impressive archway leads to the family wing of the home. The octagonal family room includes a dynamic media/fireplace wall with glass above. The mitered glass wall of the breakfast nook can be viewed from the huge island kitchen, which features a walk-in pantry and easily accesses the laundry room. A summer kitchen, perfect for outdoor grilling, is found on the covered rear patio. Two secondary bedrooms share the convenience of a Pullman-style bath and walk-in closets, and a third bedroom boasts a shared pool bath and a lovely bay window.

Sitting

Master Bedroom
16⁴ · 21⁰

Covered Patio

summer kitchen

Bath

Bedroom 5
13⁸ · 12⁰

fireplace

Family Room
20⁸ · 24⁴

w.i.c. **w.i.c.**

Bedroom 4
13⁸ · 12⁰

w.i.c.
9⁴ · 8⁰   **w.i.c.**
6⁸ · 9⁰

lin

Living Room
15⁰ · 18⁰

Breakfast

Master Bath

ac

dw

Kitchen

up

lin   **Bath**

Bedroom 3
11⁸ · 12⁴

ac

desk

seat

lin

Foyer

Dining
13⁸ · 16⁰

ref   **pantry**

w.i.c.

ac

wh

down

ac

w.i.c.

Bath

Bedroom 2
11⁸ · 16⁰

Entry

Utility
6⁸ · 10⁰

ac

up

3 Car Garage
24⁰ · 28¹⁰

Future Space
16⁰ · 32⁰

Balcony

Photos by Russell Kingman/HDS
This home, as shown in the photograph, may differ from the actual blueprints.
For more detailed information, please check the floor plans carefully.

DESIGN
HPT890002

SQUARE FOOTAGE: 2,350
WIDTH: 92'-7" DEPTH: 79'-0" L

SANTA FE STYLING CREATES INTERESTING ANGLES in this one-story home. A grand entrance leads through a courtyard into the foyer with a circular skylight, closet space, niches and a convenient powder room. Raised-hearth fireplaces in the living room, dining room and on the covered porch create a warming heart of the home. A beamed ceiling adds even more style to the living room, and an art niche sits along the edge of the dining room. The study, just to the right of the foyer, features a separate entrance and can serve as a convenient home office. Make note of the island range in the kitchen and the cozy breakfast room adjacent. The master suite has a privacy wall on the covered porch and a deluxe bath with a whirlpool tub, separate shower and private linen closet. Two more family bedrooms share a full bath—also with a whirlpool tub and linen closet—and are placed quietly in the far wing of the house near a segmented family room, which includes a storage area. Indoor/outdoor relationships are wonderful, with every room having access to the outdoors. The three-car garage offers extra storage.

Photos by Bob Greenspan
This home, as shown in the photograph, may differ from the actual blueprints.
For more detailed information, please check the floor plans carefully.

DESIGN
HPT890003

FIRST FLOOR: 2,096 SQ. FT.
SECOND FLOOR: 892 SQ. FT.
TOTAL: 2,988 SQ. FT.
STORAGE: 1,295 SQ. FT.
WIDTH: 58'-0" DEPTH: 54'-0"

THIS BEAUTIFUL VARIATION OF KEY WEST CONCH STYLE clearly emphasizes the benefits of living in a sunny clime. An abundance of windows invites warmth and light into this comfortable interior—not to mention invigorating breezes. Teeming with both vertical and horizontal lines, this home will be the darling of the neighborhood. A standing-seam roof mimics a simple balustrade and heritage columns, while louvered shutters echo the classic clapboard siding. The wraparound porch leads to a descending staircase, which eases the transition from outside to in. The two-story great room boasts a spider-beam ceiling and an entire wall of French doors that open to an entertainment lanai. Graceful arches and decorative columns define an open arrangement of the formal dining room and gourmet kitchen. This well-organized culinary paradise provides a cooktop island with food-preparation space, and a walk-in pantry. A main-level master suite has its own access to the veranda. Two walk-in closets and a dressing area announce a lavish bath with a magnificent garden tub and a wrapping vanity. On the upper level, each of two guest suites features a walk-in closet and spacious bath.

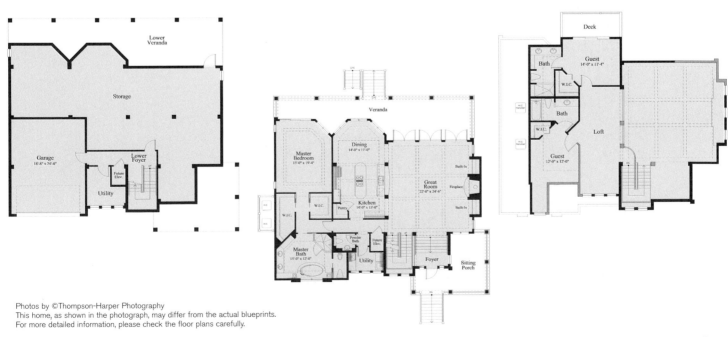

Photos by ©Thompson-Harper Photography
This home, as shown in the photograph, may differ from the actual blueprints.
For more detailed information, please check the floor plans carefully.

DESIGN
HPT890004

SQUARE FOOTAGE: 3,944
WIDTH: 98'-0" DEPTH: 105'-0" **L**

INNOVATIVE DESIGN AND ATTENTION TO DETAIL create true luxury living. This clean, contemporary-style home features a raised, columned entry with an interesting stucco relief archway. The foyer opens to the formal living room, which overlooks the lanai through walls of glass. The formal dining room has a curved wall of windows and a built-in buffet table. Two guest suites each boast a walk-in closet and a private bath. The master suite features a foyer with views of a fountain, and a sunny sitting area that opens to the lanai. The bath beckons with a soaking tub, round shower and large wardrobe area.

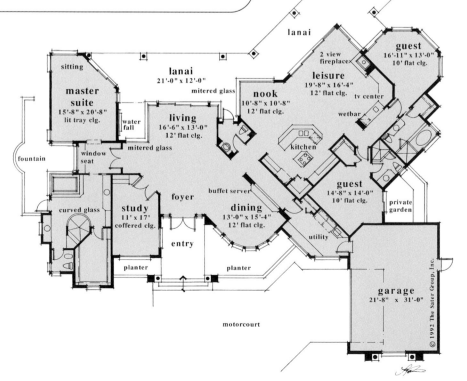

DESIGN
HPT890005

SQUARE FOOTAGE: 2,987
WIDTH: 74'-4" DEPTH: 82'-4"

CLASSIC COLUMNS, a tiled roof and beautiful arched windows herald a gracious interior for this fine home. Arched windows also mark the entrance into the vaulted living room with a tiled fireplace. The dining room opens off the vaulted foyer. Filled with light from a wall of sliding glass doors, the family room leads to the covered patio—note the wet bar and range that enhance outdoor living. The kitchen features a vaulted ceiling and unfolds into the roomy nook, which boasts French doors to the patio. The master bedroom also has patio access and shares a dual fireplace with the master bath—a solarium lights this space. A vaulted study/den sits between two additional bedrooms.

Photo by Laurence Taylor
This home, as shown in the photograph, may differ from the actual blueprints.
For more detailed information, please check the floor plans carefully.

DESIGN
HPT890006

SQUARE FOOTAGE: 3,098
BONUS SPACE: 849 SQ. FT.
WIDTH: 78'-0" DEPTH: 75'-4"

DENTILS ACCENT THE HIPPED ROOF,
while white double columns outline the
entry of this lovely three-bedroom home.
Tucked out of sight from the living room
yet close to the dining area, the island
kitchen features acres of counter space
and a convenient utility room. The breakfast nook sits open to the family room,
sharing the spacious views and warming
fireplace of this open and relaxing informal
zone. A wonderful master suite fills the
right side of the plan with luxury elements,
such as a sitting room, large walk-in closet and soaking tub. Two family bedrooms
to the left of the plan share a full bath.

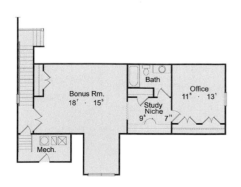

DESIGN
HPT890007

SQUARE FOOTAGE: 2,190
BASEMENT: 1,376 SQ. FT.
WIDTH: 58'-0" DEPTH: 54'-0"

A DRAMATIC SET OF STAIRS leads to the entry of this home. The foyer opens to an expansive grand room with a fireplace and built-in bookshelves. For formal meals, a front-facing dining room offers plenty of space and a bumped-out bay. The kitchen serves this area easily as well as the breakfast nook. A study and three bedrooms make up the rest of the floor plan. Two secondary bedrooms share a full bath. The master suite contains two walk-in closets and a full bath. A lower level is suitable for future recreation space.

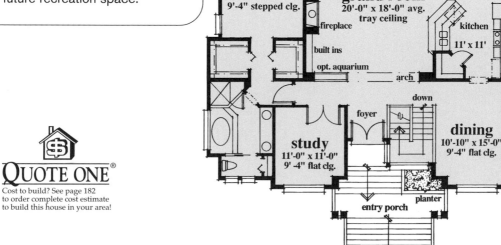

©The Sater Group, Inc.

lanai
58'-0" x 10'-8"

master suite
13'-0" x 15'-0"
9'-4" stepped clg.

built ins

grand room
20'-0" x 18'-0" avg.
tray ceiling

fireplace

built ins

opt. aquarium

arch

nook
11'-0" x 9'-4"

kitchen
11' x 11'

br. 2
12'-0" x 11'-4"
9'-4" flat clg.

utility

down

foyer

down

dining
10'-10" x 15'-0"
9'-4" flat clg.

br. 3
12'-0" x 11'-0"
9'-4" flat clg.

study
11'-0" x 11'-0"
9'-4" flat clg.

entry porch

planter

DESIGN
HPT890008

FIRST FLOOR: 2,066 SQ. FT.
SECOND FLOOR: 810 SQ. FT.
TOTAL: 2,876 SQ. FT.
BONUS SPACE: 1,260 SQ. FT.
WIDTH: 64'-0" DEPTH: 45'-0" **L**

THIS STRIKING FLORIDIAN PLAN is designed for entertaining. A large open floor plan offers soaring, sparkling space for planned gatherings. The foyer leads to the grand room, highlighted by a glass fireplace, a wet bar and wide views of the outdoors. Both the grand room and the formal dining room open to a screened veranda. The first floor includes two spacious family bedrooms and a secluded study, which opens from the grand room. The second-floor master suite offers sumptuous amenities, including a private deck and spa, a three-sided fireplace, a sizable walk-in closet and a gallery hall with an overlook to the grand room.

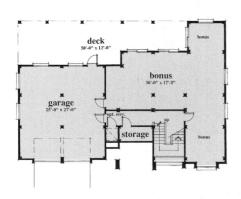

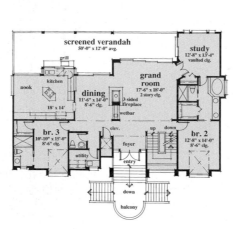

DESIGN
HPT890009

FIRST FLOOR: 1,552 SQ. FT.
SECOND FLOOR: 653 SQ. FT.
TOTAL: 2,205 SQ. FT.
WIDTH: 60'-0" DEPTH: 50'-0"

A SPLIT STAIRCASE adds flair to this European-style coastal home, where a fireplace brings warmth on chilly evenings. The foyer opens to the expansive living/dining area and island kitchen. A multitude of windows fills the interior with sunlight and ocean breezes. The wraparound rear deck finds access near the kitchen. The utility room is conveniently tucked between the kitchen and the two first-floor bedrooms. The second-floor master suite offers a private deck and a luxurious bath with a garden tub, shower and walk-in closet.

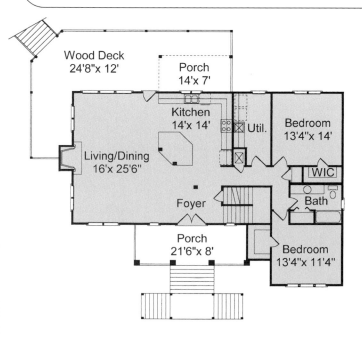

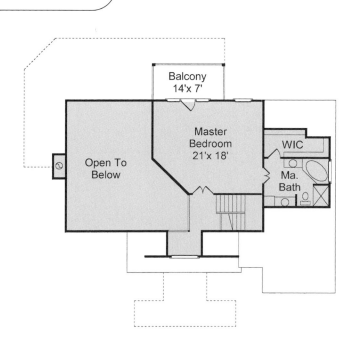

DESIGN
HPT890010

SQUARE FOOTAGE: 2,385
WIDTH: 60'-0" DEPTH: 52'-0"

THIS ENTICING EUROPEAN VILLA
boasts an Italian charm and a distinct
Mediterranean feel. The foyer steps lead
up to the formal living areas. To the left, a
study is expanded by a vaulted ceiling and
double doors that open to the front balcony. The island kitchen is conveniently
open to a breakfast nook. The guest quarters reside on the right side of the plan—
one boasts a private bath, while the second suite uses a full hall bath. The secluded master suite features two walk-in closets and a pampering whirlpool master
bath. The home is completed by a basement-level garage.

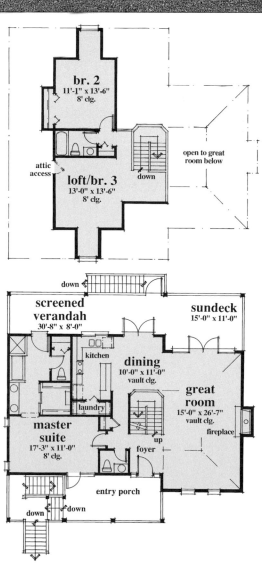

DESIGN
HPT890011

FIRST FLOOR: 1,124 SQ. FT.
SECOND FLOOR: 640 SQ. FT.
TOTAL: 1,764 SQ. FT.
WIDTH: 48'-0" DEPTH: 45'-0" **L**

AN ABUNDANCE OF PORCHES and a deck encourage year-round indoor/outdoor relationships in this classic two-story home. The spacious great room, with its cozy fireplace, and the adjacent dining room both offer access to the screened porch/deck area through French doors. The private master suite accesses both front and rear porches and leads into a relaxing private bath complete with dual vanities and a walk-in closet. An additional family bedroom and a loft/bedroom are also available.

Second Floor

br. 2
11'-1" x 13'-6"
8' clg.

attic access

loft/br. 3
13'-0" x 13'-6"
8' clg.

down

open to great room below

First Floor

down

screened verandah
30'-8" x 8'-0"

sundeck
15'-0" x 11'-0"

kitchen

dining
10'-0" x 11'-0"
vault clg.

great room
15'-0" x 26'-7"
vault clg.

fireplace

laundry

master suite
17'-3" x 11'-0"
8' clg.

up

foyer

entry porch

down down

DESIGN
HPT890012

FIRST FLOOR: 1,736 SQ. FT.
SECOND FLOOR: 640 SQ. FT.
TOTAL: 2,376 SQ. FT.
BONUS SPACE: 840 SQ. FT.
WIDTH: 54'-0" DEPTH: 44'-0" **L**

LATTICE DOOR PANELS, SHUTTERS, A BALUSTRADE AND A METAL ROOF add character to this delightful coastal home. Double doors flanking a fireplace open to the side sun deck from the spacious great room. Access to the rear veranda is also provided from this room. An adjacent dining room provides views of the rear grounds and space for formal and informal entertaining. The glassed-in nook shares space with the L-shaped kitchen containing a center work island. Bedrooms 2 and 3, a full bath and a utility room complete this floor. Upstairs, a sumptuous master suite awaits. Double doors extend to a private deck from the master bedroom. His and Hers walk-in closets lead the way to a grand bath featuring an arched whirlpool tub, a double-bowl vanity and a separate shower.

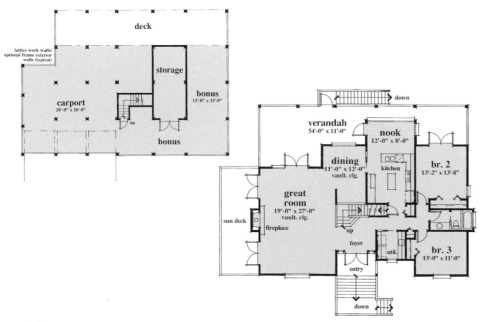

QUOTE ONE®
Cost to build? See page 182
to order complete cost estimate
to build this house in your area!

DESIGN
HPT890013

FIRST FLOOR: 1,309 SQ. FT.
SECOND FLOOR: 1,343 SQ. FT.
TOTAL: 2,652 SQ. FT.
WIDTH: 44'-4" DEPTH: 58'-2" **L**

CLEAN, CONTEMPORARY LINES, a unique floor plan and a metal roof with a cupola set this farmhouse apart. Remote-control transoms in the cupola open to create an airy and decidedly unique foyer. The great room, sun room, dining room and kitchen flow from one to another for casual entertaining with flair. The rear of the home is fashioned with plenty of windows overlooking the multi-level deck. A front bedroom and bath would make a comfortable guest suite. The master bedroom and bath upstairs are bridged by a pipe-rail balcony that also gives access to a rear deck. An additional bedroom, home office and bath complete this very special plan.

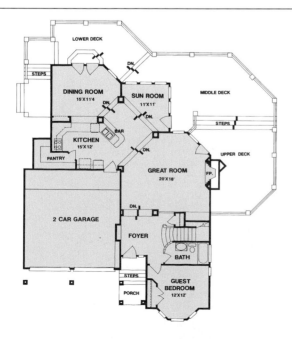

DESIGN
HPT890014

FIRST FLOOR: 1,024 SQ. FT.
SECOND FLOOR: 456 SQ. FT.
TOTAL: 1,480 SQ. FT.
WIDTH: 32'-0" DEPTH: 40'-0"

PILLARS, a large rear porch and plenty of window views lend a classic feel to this lovely country cottage. Inside, the entry room has a roomy closet and an interior entry door to eliminate drafts. The light-filled L-shaped kitchen lies conveniently near the entrance. A large room adjacent to the kitchen serves as a dining and living area where a fireplace adds warmth. A master suite boasts a walk-in closet and full bath. The second floor holds a loft, a second bedroom and full bath. This home is designed with a basement foundation.

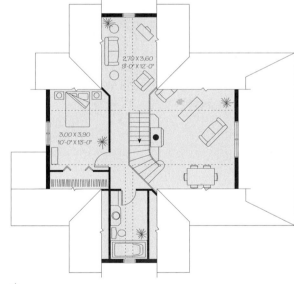

2,70 X 3,60
9'-0" X 12'-0"

3,00 X 3,90
10'-0" X 13'-0"

4,40 X 3,60
14'-8" X 12'-0"

4,20 X 6,80
14'-0" X 22'-8"

4,40 X 3,60
14'-8" X 12'-0"

DESIGN
HPT890015

FIRST FLOOR: 1,056 SQ. FT.
SECOND FLOOR: 807 SQ. FT.
TOTAL: 1,863 SQ. FT.
WIDTH: 33'-0" DEPTH: 54'-0"

WITH A TRADITIONAL FLAVOR, this fine pier design is sure to please. The living room features a fireplace and easy access to the L-shaped kitchen. Here, a work island makes meal preparation a breeze. Two family bedrooms share a full bath and access to the laundry facilities. Upstairs, a third bedroom offers a private bath and two walk-in closets. The master suite is complete with a pampering bath, two walk-in closets and a large private balcony. Please specify crawlspace or pier foundation when ordering.

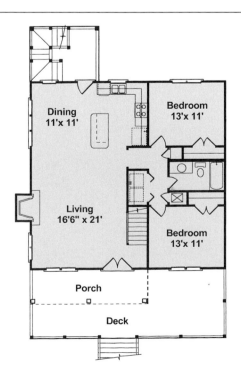

Photo by Chris A. Little of Atlanta
This home, as shown in the photograph, may differ from the actual blueprints.

DESIGN
HPT890016

FIRST FLOOR: 1,122 SQ. FT.
SECOND FLOOR: 528 SQ. FT.
TOTAL: 1,650 SQ. FT.
WIDTH: 34'-0" DEPTH: 52'-5"

THIS LOVELY SEASIDE VACATION HOME is perfect for seasonal family getaways or for the family that lives coastal year round. The spacious front deck is great for private sunbathing or outdoor barbecues, providing breathtaking ocean views. The two-story living room is warmed by a fireplace on breezy beach nights, while the island kitchen overlooks the open dining area nearby. Two first-floor family bedrooms share a hall bath. Upstairs, the master bedroom features a walk-in closet, dressing area with a vanity and access to a whirlpool tub shared with an additional family bedroom.

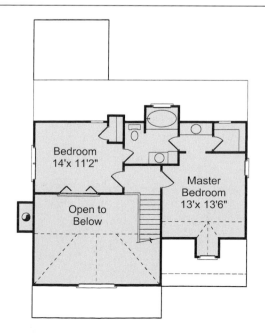

Bedroom
14'x 11'2"

Open to
Below

Master
Bedroom
13'x 13'6"

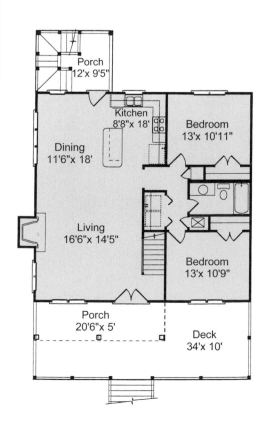

Porch
12'x 9'5"

Kitchen
8'8"x 18'

Dining
11'6"x 18'

Bedroom
13'x 10'11"

Living
16'6"x 14'5"

Bedroom
13'x 10'9"

Porch
20'6"x 5'

Deck
34'x 10'

Photo Courtesy of Chatham Home Planning, Inc.; Chris A. Little of Atlanta This home, as shown in the photograph, may differ from the actual blueprints. For more detailed information, please check the floor plans carefully.

DESIGN
HPT890017

FIRST FLOOR: 731 SQ. FT.
SECOND FLOOR: 935 SQ. FT.
TOTAL: 1,666 SQ. FT.
OTHER SPACE: 138 SQ. FT.
WIDTH: 35'-0" DEPTH: 38'-0"

THIS PIER-FOUNDATION HOME has an abundance of amenities to offer, not the least being the loft lookout. Inside, the living room is complete with a corner gas fireplace. The spacious kitchen features a cooktop island, an adjacent breakfast nook and easy access to the dining room. From this room, a set of French doors leads out to a small deck—perfect for dining alfresco. Upstairs, the sleeping zone consists of two family bedrooms sharing a full hall bath, and a deluxe master suite. Amenities in this suite include two walk-in closets and a private bath.

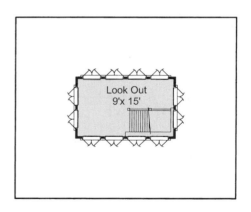

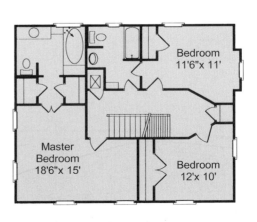

DESIGN
HPT890018

FIRST FLOOR: 1,819 SQ. FT.
SECOND FLOOR: 638 SQ. FT.
TOTAL: 2,457 SQ. FT.
BONUS SPACE: 385 SQ. FT.
WIDTH: 47'-4" DEPTH: 82'-8"

GRACEFUL DORMERS top a welcoming covered porch that is enhanced by Victorian details on this fine three-bedroom home. Inside, the foyer leads past the formal dining room back to the spacious two-story great room. Here, a fireplace, built-ins and outdoor access make any gathering special. The nearby kitchen features a work island, a pantry, a serving bar and an adjacent bayed breakfast area. Located on the first floor for privacy, the master suite is designed to pamper. Upstairs, two family bedrooms share a hall bath. Note the bonus space above the two-car garage.

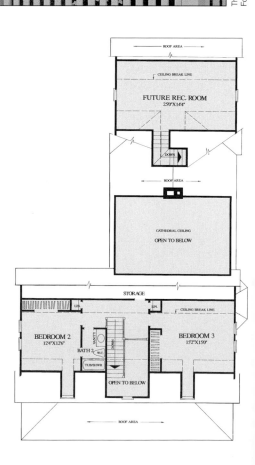

DESIGN SHOWCASE

This home, as shown in the photograph, may differ from the actual blueprints. For more detailed information, please check the floor plans carefully.

DESIGN
HPT890019

SQUARE FOOTAGE: 2,151 SQ. FT.
BONUS SPACE: 814 SQ. FT.
WIDTH: 61'-0" DEPTH: 55'-8"

THIS COUNTRY HOME has a big heart in a cozy package. Special touches—interior columns, a bay window and dormers—add elegance. The central great room features a cathedral ceiling and a fireplace. A clerestory window splashes the room with natural light. The open kitchen easily services the breakfast area and the nearby dining room. The private master bedroom, with a tray ceiling and a walk-in closet, boasts amenities found in much larger homes. The bath features a skylight and a whirlpool tub. Two additional bedrooms share a bath. The front bedroom includes a walk-in closet and would make a nice study with an optional foyer entrance.

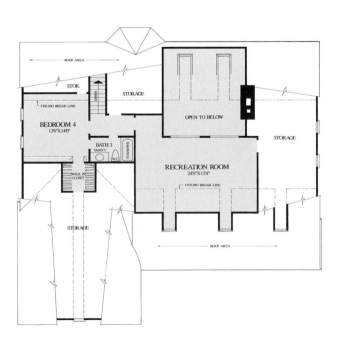

DESIGN
HPT890020

FIRST FLOOR: 2,129 SQ. FT.

SECOND FLOOR: 1,206 SQ. FT.

TOTAL: 3,335 SQ. FT.

FINISHED BASEMENT: 435 SQ. FT.

WIDTH: 59'-4" DEPTH: 64'-0"

FRENCH STYLE EMBELLISHES this dormered Southern home. Stepping through French doors to the foyer, the dining area is immediately to the left. To the right are double doors leading to a study or secondary bedroom. A lavish master bedroom provides privacy and plenty of storage space. The living room sports three doors to the rear porch and a lovely fireplace with built-ins. A secluded breakfast nook adjoins an efficient kitchen. Upstairs, two of the three family bedrooms boast dormer windows. Plans include a basement-level garage that adjoins a game room and two handy storage areas.

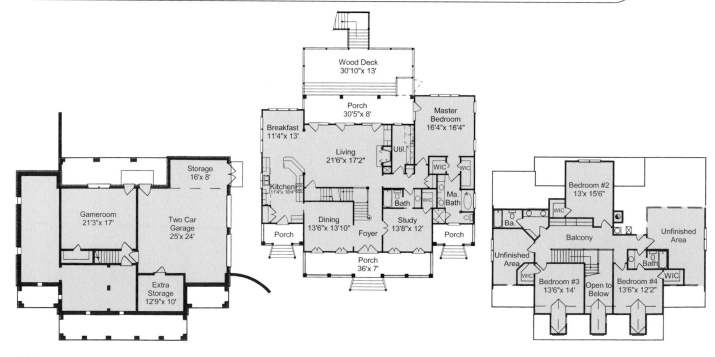

DESIGN
HPT890021

FIRST FLOOR: 1,540 SQ. FT.
SECOND FLOOR: 654 SQ. FT.
TOTAL: 2,194 SQ. FT.
WIDTH: 53'-4" DEPTH: 62'-4"

THE CAREFUL USE of vertical interior space and clerestory windows gives this three-bedroom home volume, while the floor plan makes it perfect for a narrow lot. A clerestory window in the two-level foyer combines with the cathedral ceiling in the great room and open dining room to contribute to a feeling of light and space. A smart kitchen with a cooktop/service counter serves the dining room and breakfast area. To the right of the design sits a luxurious master suite, complete with a walk-in closet, separate shower and soaking tub. Two bedrooms share a full bath on the second floor.

DESIGN
HPT890022

FIRST FLOOR: 1,356 SQ. FT.
SECOND FLOOR: 542 SQ. FT.
TOTAL: 1,898 SQ. FT.
BONUS SPACE: 393 SQ. FT.
WIDTH: 59'-0" DEPTH: 64'-0"

THE WELCOMING CHARM of this country farmhouse is expressed by its many windows and its covered wraparound porch. A two-story entrance foyer is enhanced by a Palladian window in a clerestory dormer above to let in natural lighting. The first-floor master suite allows privacy and accessibility. The master bath includes a whirlpool tub, separate shower, double-bowl vanity and walk-in closet. The first floor features nine-foot ceilings throughout with the exception of the kitchen area, which sports an eight-foot ceiling. The second floor contains two additional bedrooms, a full bath and plenty of storage space. The bonus room provides room to grow.

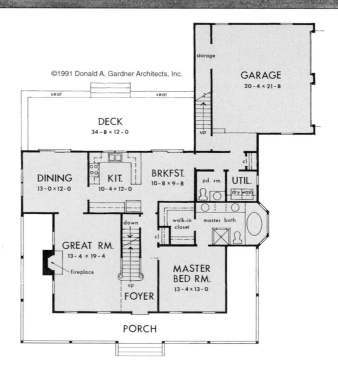

©1991 Donald A. Gardner Architects, Inc.

Quote One®
Cost to build? See page 182
to order complete cost estimate
to build this house in your area!

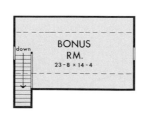

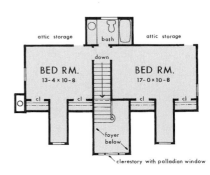

Photo courtesy of Chatham Home Planning, Inc.; Chris A. Little of Atlanta. This home, as shown in the photograph, may differ from the actual blueprints. For more detailed information, please check the floor plans carefully.

DESIGN
HPT890023

FIRST FLOOR: 1,516 SQ. FT.
SECOND FLOOR: 840 SQ. FT.
TOTAL: 2,356 SQ. FT.
WIDTH: 46'-10" DEPTH: 73'-5"

LOOKING FOR A HOME with a country attitude and modern amenities? Welcome home! A wide, columned porch graced by tall shuttered windows will greet guests with the feeling of comfort. The formal living room is enhanced by a central fireplace, while the dining room is situated just off the U-shaped kitchen. Sunshine pours in from the breakfast area, flooding the kitchen with light. The master bedroom features a walk-in closet and double doors to the dual-vanity bathroom. Upstairs, three family bedrooms—two enjoy walk-in closets—share a compartmented bath. The rear-loading, two-car garage doesn't detract from the symmetry of the home.

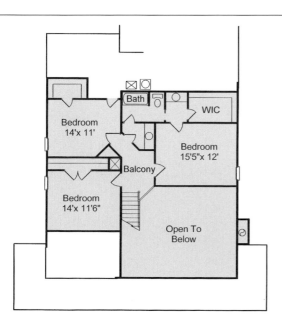

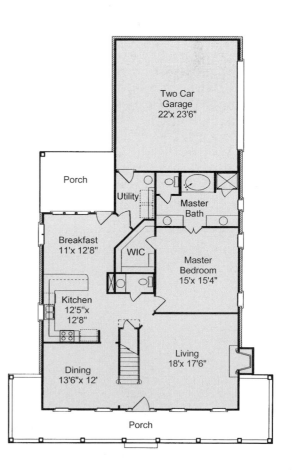

DESIGN
HPT890024

FIRST FLOOR: 576 SQ. FT.
SECOND FLOOR: 576 SQ. FT.
TOTAL: 1,152 SQ. FT.
WIDTH: 24'-0" DEPTH: 24'-0"

THIS COZY LAKEFRONT vacation home is great for the small family or retired couple. Double doors open into a combined kitchen/dining/living room area, large enough for family gatherings. A powder room is located at the rear of the plan, where a staircase leads to the second floor. Upstairs, a loft/sitting area easily converts to additional sleeping quarters just outside of the master suite. This large master bedroom provides a roomy walk-in closet and private access to a petite front balcony with spacious views. The sitting area and master bedroom share access to a second-floor full bath that includes a corner soaking tub and separate shower. This home is designed with a basement foundation.

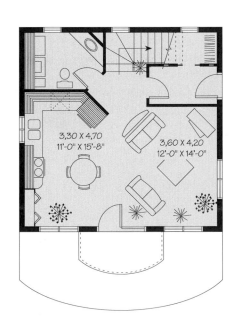

3,30 X 4,70
11'-0" X 15'-8"

3,60 X 4,20
12'-0" X 14'-0"

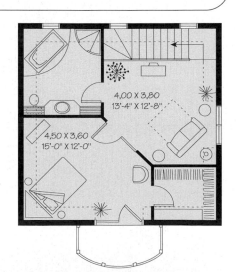

4,00 X 3,80
13'-4" X 12'-8"

4,50 X 3,60
15'-0" X 12'-0"

DESIGN
HPT890025

FIRST FLOOR: 1,075 SQ. FT.
SECOND FLOOR: 994 SQ. FT.
TOTAL: 2,069 SQ. FT.
BONUS SPACE: 382 SQ. FT.
WIDTH: 56'-4" DEPTH: 35'-4"

THIS COTTAGE DESIGN calls for the calming sounds of water and the easiness of sunshine-filled days. Stacked covered porches make fine spots for relaxation and offer beautiful outdoor extensions for entertaining. The great room features a comfortable fireplace and access to a rear porch. To the left are an island kitchen and casual breakfast nook. Upstairs, the master bedroom is complete with dual-vanities, compartmented toilet, separate tub and shower and connecting His and Hers walk-in closets. Two family bedrooms share a Jack-and-Jill bath. A future recreation space is ideal for a game room or media space.

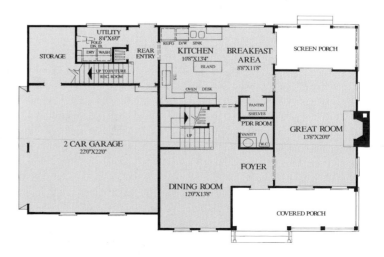

DESIGN
HPT890026

SQUARE FOOTAGE: 3,144
WIDTH: 139'-10" DEPTH: 63'-8" **L**

IN CLASSIC SOUTHWESTERN STYLE, this home strikes a beautiful balance between preserving the historic integrity of its classic style and the open spirit of a contemporary interior. A covered porch runs the width of the front exterior and extends the living areas to the outdoors. A rambling family kitchen invites casual gatherings and lively conversations. To the right of the plan, two family bedrooms share a full bath and look out to the rear property and terrace. The master suite—complete with its own fireplace—enjoys privacy nestled in a quiet wing it shares with a study, which could double as a guest room. The master bath offers a corner whirlpool tub, twin vanity sinks and a separate shower.

Cost to build? See page 182
to order complete cost estimate
to build this house in your area!

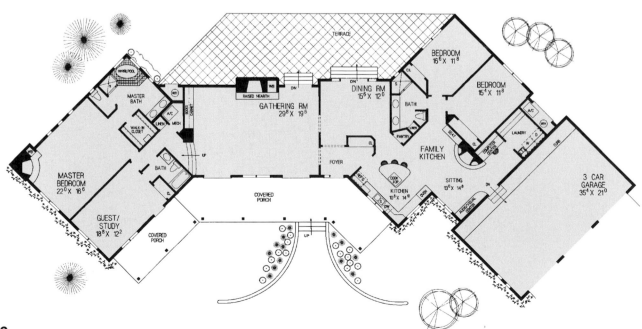

DESIGN
HPT890027

SQUARE FOOTAGE: 3,163
WIDTH: 75'-2" DEPTH: 68'-8"

AN OPEN COURTYARD takes center stage in this home, providing a happy marriage of indoor/outdoor relationships. Art collectors will appreciate the gallery that enhances the entry and showcases their favorite works. The centrally located great room supplies the nucleus for formal and informal entertaining. A raised-hearth fireplace flanked by built-in media centers adds a special touch. The master suite provides a private retreat where you may relax—try the sitting room or retire to the private bath for a pampering soak in the corner whirlpool tub.

QUOTE ONE®
Cost to build? See page 182
to order complete cost estimate
to build this house in your area!

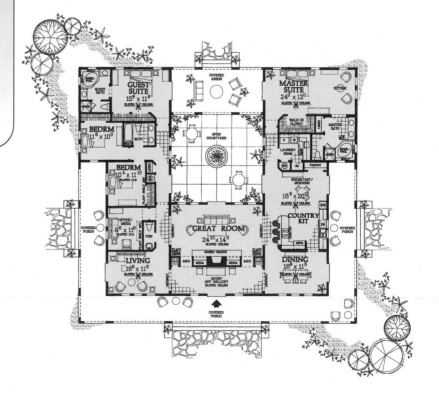

DESIGN
HPT890028

TOTAL: 2,262 SQ. FT.
LIVING BASEMENT: 1,822 SQ. FT.
WIDTH: 109'-11" DEPTH: 46'-0"

THIS EXQUISITE HOME is definitely Mediterranean, with its corner quoins, lintels and tall entry. This home features a dining room, a massive family room with a fireplace, a gourmet kitchen with a breakfast area and a laundry room. Finishing the first floor is a lavish master suite, which enjoys a vast walk-in closet, a sitting area and a pampering private bath. The lower level features three suites, two full baths, a pool room and a recreation room/theater along with two storage rooms.

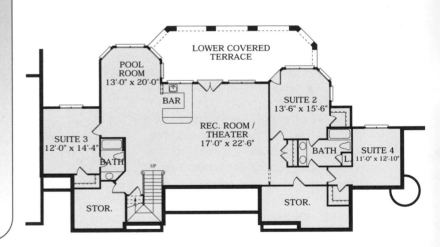

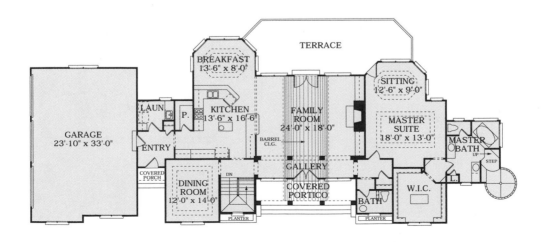

DESIGN
HPT890029

SQUARE FOOTAGE: 2,747
FINISHED BASEMENT: 1,735 SQ. FT.
WIDTH: 74'-4" DEPTH: 83'-2"

THE TOWERING ENTRY of this stucco beauty makes for a gracious entrance to the floor plan inside. Double doors open off the covered front porch to a dining room and a living room defined by columns. A fireplace warms the living room. To the back are the casual areas: a family room, breakfast nook and gourmet kitchen. A bedroom with a full bath and the utility area sit directly behind the two-car garage. The master suite features a study and private bath. The lower level can be developed into a recreation room or additional bedroom suites.

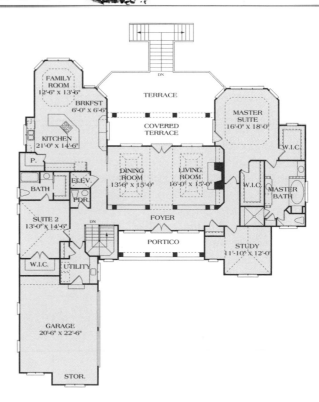

DESIGN
HPT890030

SQUARE FOOTAGE: 2,831
WIDTH: 84'-0" DEPTH: 77'-0" [L]

BESIDES GREAT CURB APPEAL, this home has a wonderful floor plan. The foyer features a fountain that greets visitors and leads to a formal dining room on the right and a living room on the left. A large family room at the rear has a built-in entertainment center and a fireplace. The U-shaped kitchen is perfectly located for servicing all living and dining areas. To the right of the plan, away from the central entertaining spaces, are three family bedrooms sharing a full bath. On the left side, with solitude and comfort for the master suite, are a large sitting area, an office and an amenity-filled bath. A deck with a spa sits outside the master suite.

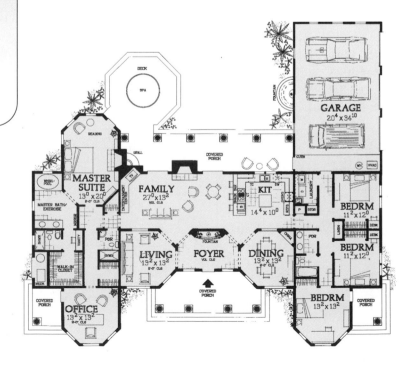

DESIGN
HPT890031

SQUARE FOOTAGE: 3,018
WIDTH: 74'-0" DEPTH: 82'-0"

TWO DISTINCT EXTERIORS can be built from the details for this plan—both are perfect as Sun Country designs. The grand entry allows for a twelve-foot ceiling in the entry foyer. Open planning calls for columns to separate the formal living and dining rooms from the foyer and central hall. Both rooms have tray ceilings, and the living room has a fireplace and double-door access to the skylit lanai. The modified U-shaped kitchen opens to an attached breakfast room and steps down to the family room with its fireplace and optional wet bar. A lovely octagonal foyer introduces family bedrooms and their private baths. Separated from family bedrooms, the master suite offers double-door access to the rear yard, a walk-in closet and a full bath with a whirlpool tub, double vanity, compartmented toilet and separate shower.

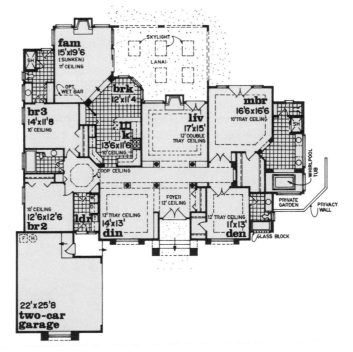

REAR ELEVATION

ALTERNATE ELEVATION

DESIGN
HPT890032

SQUARE FOOTAGE: 3,656
WIDTH: 102'-4" DEPTH: 102'-4"

AN INTRIGUING ITALIAN villa-style design offers a luxurious layout for the family that entertains. The grand entry focuses on the flow from living room to dining room—splendid for large groups of guests. A private study provides solitude for reading or business. Nearby, the master suite is a work in the fine art of relaxation. Surrounding the master bath, a secluded garden offers a soothing landscape. An oversize walk-in closet enhances storage needs while the main bedroom is embellished with a stepped ceiling and access to the extensive rear veranda. At the opposite end of the home, a spacious leisure room, nook and kitchen serve up casual atmosphere for the family. Secondary bedrooms can be found along the gallery—each with its own full bath and walk-in closet.

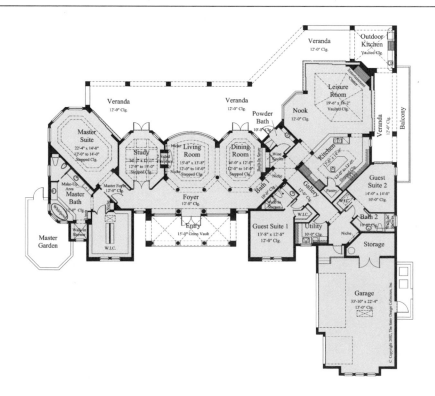

DESIGN
HPT890033

SQUARE FOOTAGE: 3,244
WIDTH: 90'-0"   DEPTH: 105'-0"

A HIGH HIPPED ROOF and contemporary fanlight windows set the tone for this elegant plan. The grand foyer opens to the formal dining and living rooms, which are set apart with arches, highlighted with art niches and framed with walls of windows. Featuring a gourmet kitchen, breakfast nook and leisure room with a built-in entertainment center, the living area has full view of and access to the lanai. Secondary bedrooms are privately situated through a gallery hall, and both include private baths and walk-in closets. The main wing houses a full study and a master bedroom with a private garden.

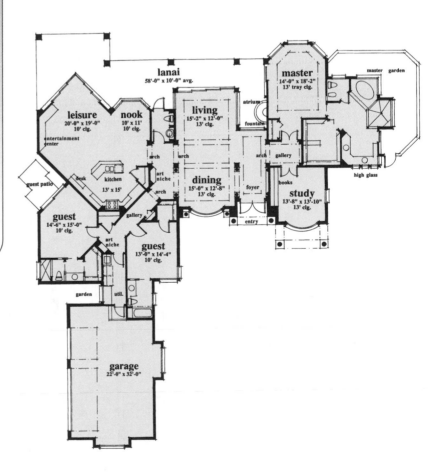

DESIGN
HPT890034

SQUARE FOOTAGE: 2,319
WIDTH: 97'-2" DEPTH: 57'-4"

THE TILED FOYER of this Sun Country design invites guests into a gathering room with a fireplace and views of the rear grounds. Half-walls define the formal dining area, which offers rear-patio access. The kitchen is equipped to serve formal and informal occasions, and includes a snack counter for meals on the go. An office or guest room has a sunny bay window and an adjacent powder room. The outstanding master suite contains twin walk-in closets, a whirlpool tub, a sit-down vanity and a stylish doorless shower. Two secondary bedrooms share a bath.

QUOTE ONE®
Cost to build? See page 182
to order complete cost estimate
to build this house in your area!

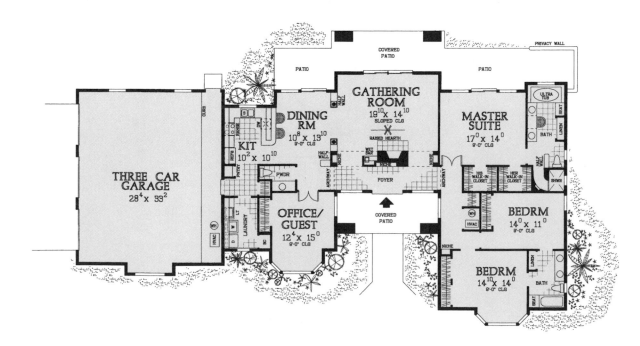

DESIGN
HPT890035

SQUARE FOOTAGE: 2,503
WIDTH: 60'-0" DEPTH: 78'-4"

SQUARE PILLARS ELEGANTLY introduce the entry of this gracious three-bedroom home. Past the two-door entry, a
Mediterranean-style family room impress-
es guests. The built-in entertainment center surrounding the fireplace enhances the
spacious feel of the living room. To the
right resides a master suite with a sunny
sitting area, two walk-in closets, private
access to the rear covered porch, and a
master bath featuring a soaking tub set in
a concave wall of glass. To the left of the
design are the two family bedrooms—note
the walk-in closets and private baths for
each room!—a kitchen, bayed breakfast
nook and handy utility room. This home
would be perfect for placement on or near
a golf course—the plan includes its own
golf-cart garage door.

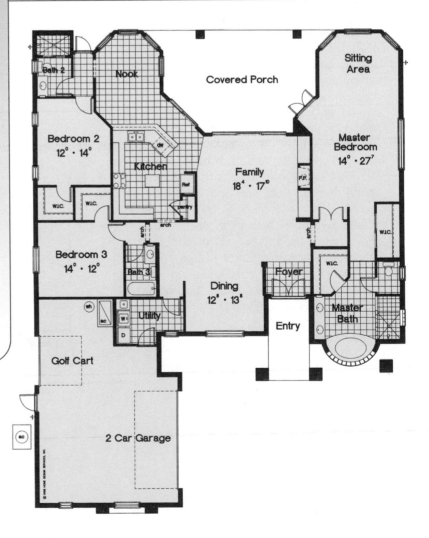

© 1994 Donald A. Gardner Architects, Inc.

B. NATHAN

DESIGN
HPT890036

SQUARE FOOTAGE: 1,838
WIDTH: 60'-0" DEPTH: 60'-4"

ARCHED WINDOWS and a dramatic arched entry enhance this exciting contemporary home. The expansive great room, highlighted by a cathedral ceiling and a fireplace, offers direct access to the rear patio and the formal dining room—a winning combination for both formal and informal get-togethers. An efficient U-shaped kitchen provides plenty of counter space and easily serves both the dining room and the great room. Sunlight fills the master bedroom through a wall of windows, which affords views of the rear grounds. The master bath invites relaxation with its soothing corner tub and separate shower. Two secondary bedrooms (one serves as an optional study) share an adjacent bath.

© 1994 Donald A. Gardner Architects, Inc.

DESIGN
HPT890037

SQUARE FOOTAGE: 2,952
WIDTH: 70'-0" DEPTH: 98'-0" L

CLASSIC COLUMNS, circle-head windows and a bay-windowed study give this stucco home a wonderful street presence. The foyer leads to the formal living and dining areas. An arched buffet server separates these rooms and contributes an open feeling. The kitchen, nook and leisure room are grouped for informal living. A desk/message center in the island kitchen, art niches in the nook and a fireplace with an entertainment center and shelves add custom touches. Two secondary suites have guest baths and offer full privacy from the master wing. The master suite hosts a private garden area, while the master bath features a walk-in shower that overlooks the garden, and a water-closet room with space for books or a television. Large His and Hers walk-in closets complete these private quarters.

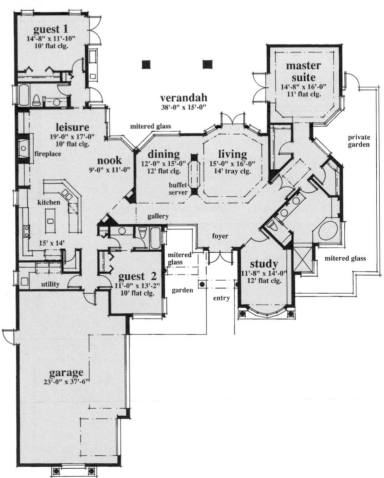

DESIGN
HPT890038

SQUARE FOOTAGE: 2,774
BONUS SPACE: 493 SQ. FT.
WIDTH: 65'-4" DEPTH: 85'-10"

A VERY EFFICIENT PLAN that minimizes the use of enclosed hallways creates a very open feeling of space and orderliness. As you enter the foyer you have a clear view through the spacious living room to the covered patio beyond. The formal dining area is to the right and the master wing is to the left. The master bedroom boasts a sitting area, access to the patio, His and Hers walk-in closets, dual vanities, a walk-in shower and a compartmented toilet. A large island kitchen overlooks the nook and family room, which has a built-in media/fireplace wall. Three additional bedrooms and two full baths complete the plan.

DESIGN
HPT890039

SQUARE FOOTAGE: 3,074
WIDTH: 77'-0" DEPTH: 66'-8"

THIS STUNNING PARADISE achieves its casual European character by mixing Spanish and French influences. A fanlight transom caps the stately entry and speaks volumes about timeless beauty. The dazzling portico leads to a mid-level foyer and to the grand salon—a magnificent room of graceful arches and endless views. True to its character, the home blurs the line between indoors and out with walls of glass and an extensive covered porch. Views of nature mix with the glow of an inglenook hearth in the leisure room, where family members and close friends can gather. Two guest suites provide accommodations for visiting relatives and friends. Each of the suites offers a private bath and walk-in closet. A gallery hall connects the suites and leads to a convenient laundry and lower-level staircase. The master wing opens to a private area of the rear covered porch. Nearby, a cabana-style powder room opens to the porch and to the homeowner's private hall. Pocket doors to the study provide a quiet place for reading, surfing and quiet conversations.

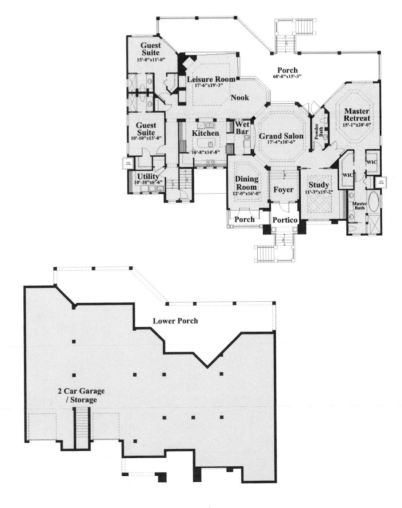

DESIGN
HPT890040

SQUARE FOOTAGE: 1,929
WIDTH: 59'-0" DEPTH: 68'-8"

MAKE THE MOST of warmer climes in this striking three-bedroom home. A grand entry gives way to a great room with skylights and a fireplace. A cathedral ceiling furthers the feeling of spaciousness in this room. A large dining room surveys views on two sides. Adjacent, the kitchen will delight with its large island work space and abundance of counter and cabinet space. The breakfast room offers ample space along with elegant ceiling detail. Three bedrooms—or two bedrooms and a study—make up the sleeping quarters of this plan. The master suite offers a private bath with dual sinks, a walk-in closet and a bumped-out garden tub. A secluded covered porch provides the opportunity for outdoor enjoyment.

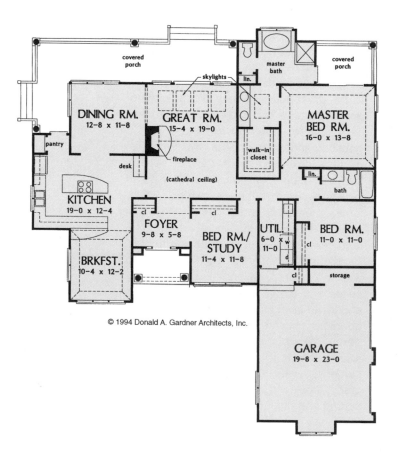

DESIGN
HPT890041

SQUARE FOOTAGE: 2,612
WIDTH: 93'-7" DEPTH: 74'-10" **L**

DRAMATIC INTERIOR ANGLES provide for an immensely livable plan that is metered with elegance enough for any social occasion. The open passage to the living room and formal dining room from the foyer is perfect for entertaining, while casual areas are positioned to the rear of the plan. The spacious kitchen, with extra storage at every turn, has an eat-in nook and a door to the rear patio. Two family bedrooms share a hall bath to complete this wing. The master suite is split from the family area to ensure a private retreat. The large bedroom can easily accommodate a sitting area and has a luxurious bath, walk-in closet and sliding doors to a private patio.

QUOTE ONE®
Cost to build? See page 182
to order complete cost estimate
to build this house in your area!

DESIGN
HPT890042

SQUARE FOOTAGE: 2,656
WIDTH: 92'-0" DEPTH: 69'-0"

A GRACEFUL DESIGN sets this charming home apart from the ordinary and transcends the commonplace. From the foyer, the dining room branches off the sunny living room, setting a lovely backdrop for entertaining. Casual living is the focus in the oversized family room, where sliding doors open to the patio and the eat-in, gourmet kitchen is open for easy conversation. Two family bedrooms and a cabana bath are just off the family room. The master suite has a cozy fireplace in the sitting area, and twin closets and a compartmented bath. A large covered patio adds to the living area.

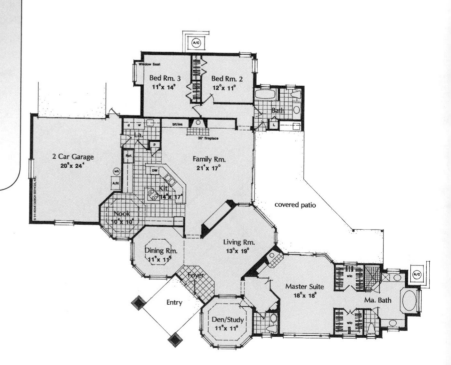

DESIGN
HPT890043

SQUARE FOOTAGE: 2,089
WIDTH: 61'-8" DEPTH: 50'-4"

THIS FOUR-BEDROOM, three-bath home offers the finest in modern amenities. The huge family room, which opens up to the patio with twelve-foot pocket sliding doors, provides space for a fireplace and media equipment. Two family bedrooms share a full bath while one bedroom has a private bath with patio access, making it the perfect guest room. The master suite, located just off the kitchen and nook, is private yet easily accessible. The double-door entry, bed wall with glass above, the step-down shower and private toilet room, walk-in linen closet and lavish vanity make this a very comfortable master suite!

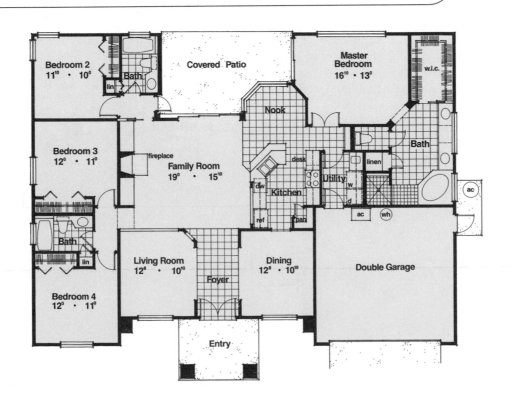

DESIGN
HPT890044

SQUARE FOOTAGE: 1,954
WIDTH: 64'-10" DEPTH: 58'-10"

DIRECT FROM THE MEDITERRANEAN, this Spanish-style, one-story home offers a practical floor plan. The facade features arch-top, multi-pane windows, a columned front porch, a tall chimney and a tiled roof. The interior has a wealth of livability. What you'll appreciate first is the juxtaposition of the great room and the formal dining room—both defined by columns. A more casual eating area is attached to the L-shaped kitchen and accesses a screened porch, as does the great room. Three bedrooms mean abundant sleeping space. The study could be a fourth bedroom—choose the full bath option in this case. A tray ceiling decorates the master suite, which is further enhanced by a bath with a separate shower and tub, walk-in closet and double sinks.

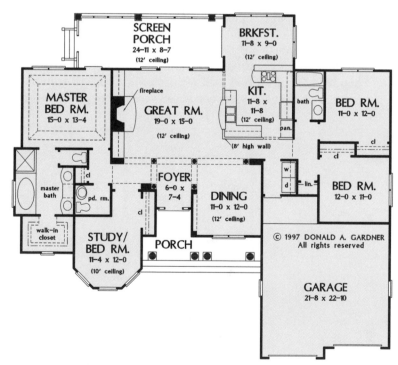

(optional full bath)

DESIGN
HPT890045

SQUARE FOOTAGE: 2,660
WIDTH: 66'-4" DEPTH: 74'-4"

CIRCLE-TOP WINDOWS are beautifully showcased in this magnificent home. The double-door entry leads into the foyer and welcomes guests into a formal living and dining room area with wonderful views. As you approach the entrance to the master suite, you pass the den/study, which can easily become a guest or bedroom suite. A gently bowed soffit and stepped ceiling treatments add excitement to the master bedroom, with floor-length windows framing the bed. The bay-window sitting area further enhances the opulence of the suite. The master bath comes complete with a double vanity, a make-up area and a soaking tub balanced by the large shower and private toilet chamber. The walk-in closet caps off this well-appointed space with ample hanging and built-in areas.

DESIGN
HPT890046

SQUARE FOOTAGE: 1,674
WIDTH: 68'-0" DEPTH: 48'-8" L D

STUCCOED ARCHES, multi-paned windows and a gracefully sloped roof accent the exterior of this Spanish-inspired design. The front foyer leads to each of the living areas: a sloped-ceiling gathering room, a study (or optional bedroom), a formal dining room and the light-filled breakfast room. Bedrooms are in a wing to the left and feature a master suite with a walk-in closet and terrace access. A covered porch opens off the dining room for private outdoor meals. The two-car garage is made even more useful with a large storage area—or use it for workshop space.

Cost to build? See page 182 to order complete cost estimate to build this house in your area!

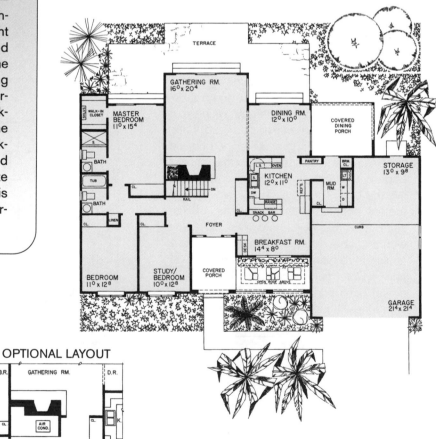

OPTIONAL LAYOUT

DESIGN
HPT890047

MAIN LEVEL: 1,530 SQ. FT.
UPPER LEVEL: 984 SQ. FT.
LOWER LEVEL: 951 SQ. FT.
TOTAL: 3,465 SQ. FT.
WIDTH: 90'-0" DEPTH: 56'-0" **L** **D**

THE ENTRY COURT of this design features planter areas and a small pool. Down six steps from the foyer is the lower level, housing a bedroom and full bath, a study and an activities room. Upper-level sleeping quarters are located six steps up from the foyer. The main level accommodates the living areas: formal living room, kitchen and adjoining breakfast room, powder room and laundry room. A three-car garage allows plenty of room for the family fleet.

QUOTE ONE®
Cost to build? See page 182
to order complete cost estimate
to build this house in your area!

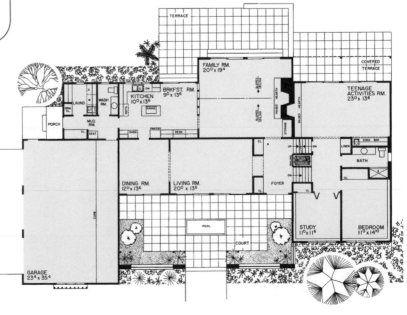

DESIGN
HPT890048

SQUARE FOOTAGE: 2,430
WIDTH: 70'-2" DEPTH: 53'-0"

WITH A ROW OF PRETTY WINDOWS, this gentle Mediterranean home offers plenty of views and outdoor spaces for mingling with nature. High ceilings in the great room and dining room extend the sense of spaciousness and propose planned events that spill out to the outdoor spaces. The formal dining room opens through a colonnade from the central gallery hall and shares the comfort of the central fireplace. A food-preparation island and service counter allow easy meals or fabulous dinners. Of course, the best part of the eating area is the morning nook—a bright reprieve from daily cares surrounded with the beauty of sunshine and trees.

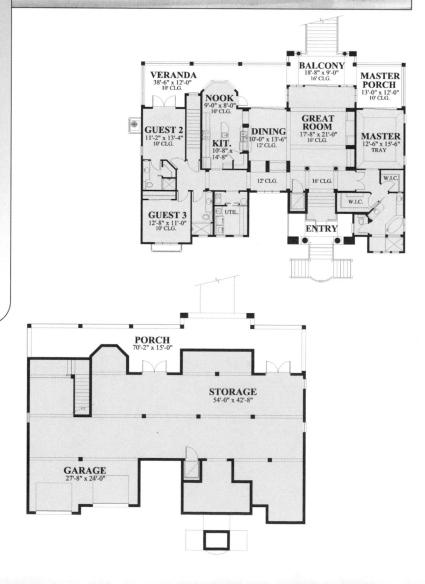

DESIGN
HPT890049

FIRST FLOOR: 2,853 SQ. FT.
SECOND FLOOR: 627 SQ. FT.
TOTAL: 3,480 SQ. FT.
GUEST HOUSE: 312 SQ. FT.
WIDTH: 80'-0" DEPTH: 96'-0" L

A UNIQUE COURTYARD provides a happy marriage of indoor/outdoor relationships for this design. Inside, the foyer opens to a grand salon with a wall of glass, providing unobstructed views of the backyard. Informal areas include a leisure room with an entertainment center and glass doors that open to a covered poolside lanai. An outdoor fireplace enhances casual gatherings. The master suite is filled with amenities that include a bayed sitting area, access to the rear lanai, His and Hers closets and a soaking tub. Upstairs, two family bedrooms—both with private decks—share a full bath. A detached guest house has a cabana bath and an outdoor grill area.

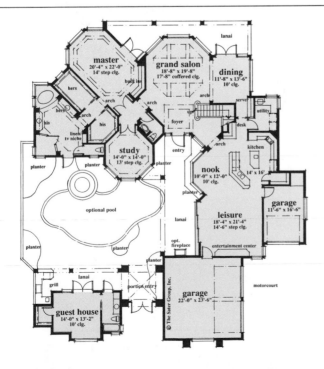

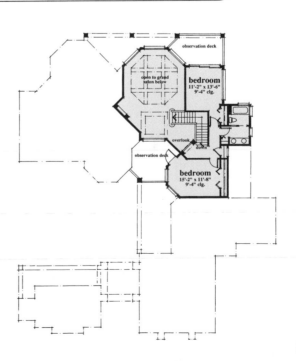

DESIGN
HPT890050

SQUARE FOOTAGE: 1,715
WIDTH: 55'-0" DEPTH: 49'-0"

A GRAND DOUBLE BANK of windows looking in on the formal dining room mirrors the lofty elegance of the extra-tall vaulted ceiling inside. From the foyer, an arched entrance to the great room visually frames the fireplace on the back wall. The wraparound kitchen has plenty of counter and cabinet space, along with a handy serving bar. The luxurious master suite features a front sitting room for quiet times and a large spa-style bath. Two family bedrooms share a hall bath. Please specify basement, slab or crawlspace foundation when ordering.

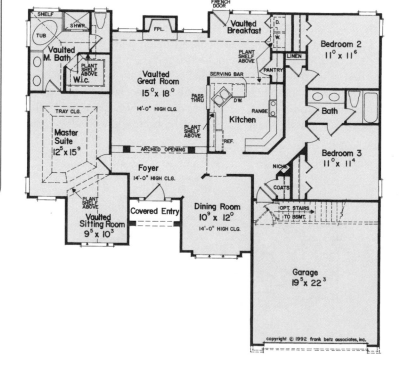

QUOTE ONE®

Cost to build? See page 182
to order complete cost estimate
to build this house in your area!

DESIGN
HPT890051

SQUARE FOOTAGE: 1,784
WIDTH: 58'-0" DEPTH: 64'-8" [L]

THIS ONE-STORY HOME is filled with amenities. A raised entry features double doors that lead to the grand foyer. From the formal living room, large sliding glass doors open to the lanai, providing natural light and outdoor views. The dining room is separated from the foyer and living area by a half-wall and a column. The large kitchen, breakfast nook and leisure room round out the informal gathering areas. The secondary bedrooms are split from the master wing. The cozy master suite sports a large walk-in closet, walk-in shower, whirlpool tub and private water closet.

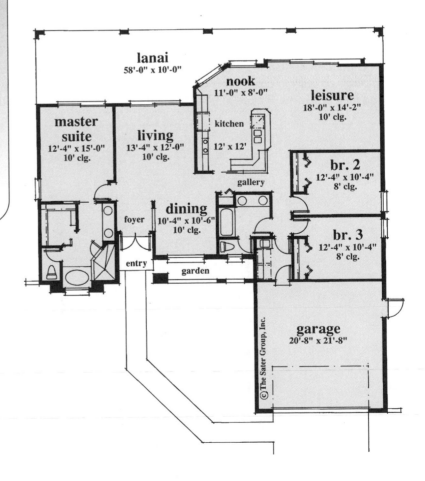

DESIGN
HPT890052

SQUARE FOOTAGE: 2,046
WIDTH: 68'-2" DEPTH: 57'-4"

A SIX-PANEL DOOR with an arched transom makes an impressive entry. Upon entering the foyer, the formal dining room resides to the right. The great room comes complete with a cozy fireplace and built-ins. On the far left of the home, two bedrooms share a full bath and a linen closet. The kitchen and breakfast room provide an ample amount of space for the family to enjoy meals together. The rear porch is also accessible from a rear bedroom and from an angled door between the great room and breakfast room. In the master bedroom, two walk-in closets provide plenty of space and two separate vanities make dressing less crowded. Please specify basement, crawlspace or slab foundation when ordering.

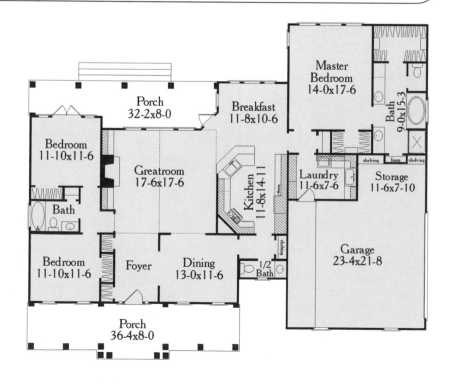

DESIGN
HPT890053

SQUARE FOOTAGE: 1,288
WIDTH: 32'-4" DEPTH: 60'-0"

WELCOME HOME to casual, unstuffy living with this comfortable tidewater design. The heart of this home is the great room, where a put-your-feet-up atmosphere prevails, and the dusky hues of sunset can mingle with the sounds of ocean breakers. The efficient kitchen is centrally located, making serving to the dining room or great room a breeze. French doors open the master suite to a private area of the covered porch, where sunlight and sea breezes mingle with a spirit of bon vivant.

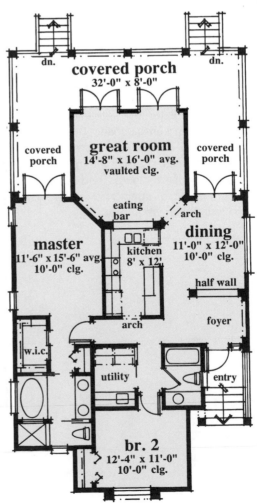

DESIGN
HPT890054

SQUARE FOOTAGE: 2,111
WIDTH: 49'-0" DEPTH: 74'-0"

HIPPED AND GABLED ROOFLINES combine with fine stucco detailing on this welcoming three-bedroom home. Inside, the foyer is flanked by a hall way to the secondary bedrooms on the left and an octagonal eating area to the right. The spacious family room features a fireplace, built-ins and screen-porch access. The angled kitchen easily serves the formal and informal dining areas. A lavish master suite features two walk-in closets and a sumptuous bath. Please specify crawl-space or slab foundation when ordering.

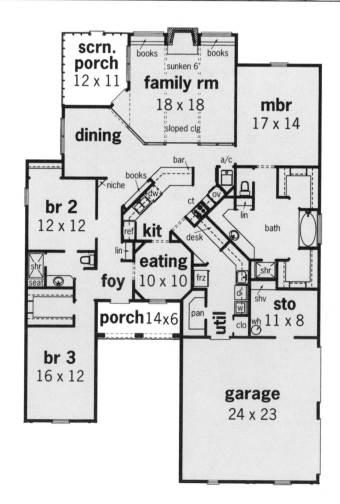

DESIGN
HPT890055

FIRST FLOOR: 3,058 SQ. FT.
SECOND FLOOR: 279 SQ. FT.
TOTAL: 3,337 SQ. FT.
WIDTH: 104'-6" DEPTH: 58'-4" **L**

A CENTRALLY LOCATED INTERIOR ATRIUM is just one of the interesting features of this Spanish design. The atrium has a built-in seat and will bring light to the adjacent living room, dining room and breakfast room. Beyond the foyer and down one step, a tiled reception hall includes a powder room. This area leads to the sleeping wing and up one step to the family room with its raised-hearth fireplace and sliding glass doors to the rear terrace. Overlooking the family room is a railed lounge that can be used for various activities. Sleeping areas include a deluxe master suite and three family bedrooms.

Quote One®
Cost to build? See page 182
to order complete cost estimate
to build this house in your area!

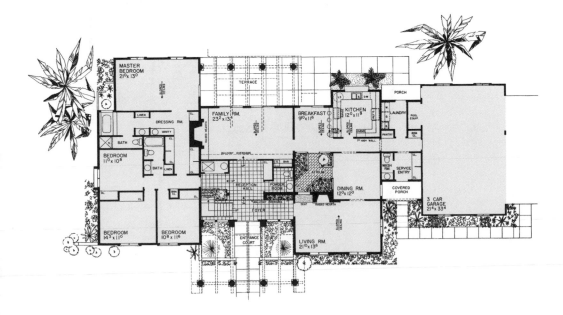

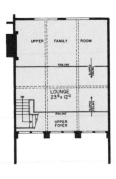

DESIGN
HPT890056

SQUARE FOOTAGE: 2,454
WIDTH: 66'-8" DEPTH: 56'-8"

THIS ONE-STORY HOME sports many well-chosen, distinctive exterior details including a cameo window and hipped rooflines. The dining and living rooms flank the foyer. A tray ceiling in the living room adds further enhancement. The bayed breakfast area admits light softened by the patio. Secluded from the main portion of the house, the master bedroom features a tray ceiling and a through-fireplace to the private bath. A raised tub, double vanity and immense walk-in closet highlight the bath.

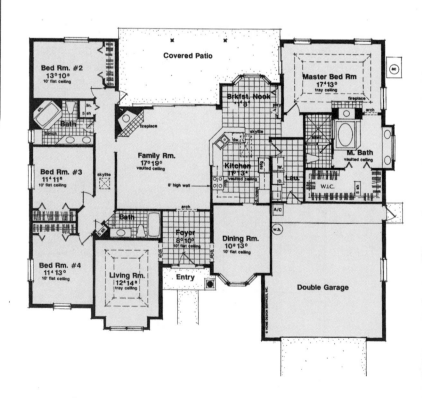

DESIGN
HPT890057

SQUARE FOOTAGE: 2,253
WIDTH: 58'-0" DEPTH: 66'-8"

THE FUNCTIONAL USE of angles in this house make for a plan that is exciting and full of large spaces. A formal living/dining area greets guests as they enter. The mitered glass throughout the rear of the home creates unlimited views to the outdoor living space and pool. Double doors lead to the master suite. A grand bath here boasts His and Hers walk-in closets, a wraparound vanity, a corner tub and a shower. The best feature of this home is the split-bedroom design. It contains a bedroom that has a private bath, perfect for guest or family-member visits. The remaining two bedrooms share their own bath off the hall.

DESIGN
HPT890058

FIRST FLOOR: 2,058 SQ. FT.
SECOND FLOOR: 712 SQ. FT.
TOTAL: 2,770 SQ. FT.
WIDTH: 57'-3"   DEPTH: 81'-3"

IF YOU'VE ALWAYS DREAMED of owning a villa, we invite you to experience this European lifestyle—on a perfectly manageable scale. This home offers the best of traditional formality and casual elegance. The foyer leads to the great room, with a bold but stylish fireplace and three French doors to the rear terrace—sure to be left open during fair weather. The large kitchen opens gracefully to a private dining room that has access to a covered outdoor patio. The master suite combines great views and a sumptuous bath to complete this winning design. Upstairs, a balcony hall overlooking the great room leads to two family bedrooms that share a full hall bath.

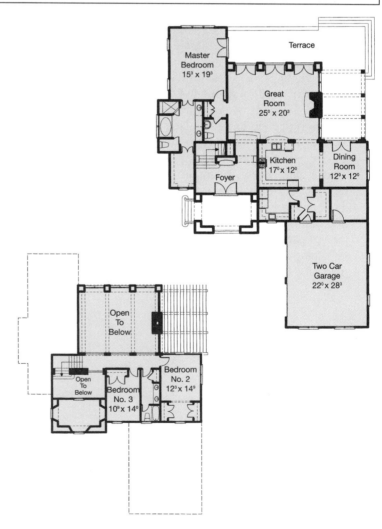

DESIGN
HPT890059

FIRST FLOOR: 1,475 SQ. FT.
SECOND FLOOR: 1,460 SQ. FT.
TOTAL: 2,935 SQ. FT.
WIDTH: 57'-6"   DEPTH: 46'-6"

FRENCH-ENTRY DOORS open to a formal dining room on the left with excellent frontal views, and a formal living room on the right that leads to a quiet corner media room. The bayed great room offers access to the rear deck in order to enjoy the full benefits of sun and outdoor activities. A large island kitchen with a bayed breakfast nook completes the first floor of this plan. Upstairs, Bedrooms 2 and 3 share a full bath, while Bedroom 4 includes its own bath. The master bedroom features a bayed sitting area and an exquisite bath with a wonderful vanity area, massive walk-in closet and unique step-up tub. This home is designed with a walkout basement foundation.

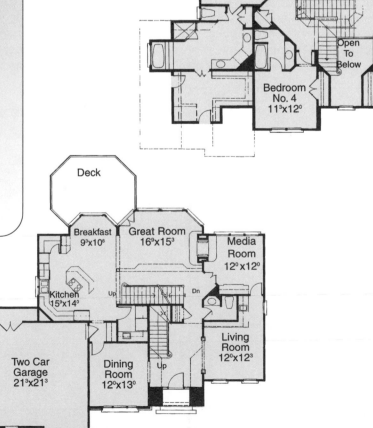

DESIGN
HPT890060

FIRST FLOOR: 1,305 SQ. FT.
SECOND FLOOR: 1,215 SQ. FT.
TOTAL: 2,520 SQ. FT.
BONUS SPACE: 935 SQ. FT.
WIDTH: 30'-6" DEPTH: 72'-2"

LOUVERED SHUTTERS, BALUSTERED RAILINGS AND A SLATE-STYLE ROOF complement a stucco-and-siding blend on this narrow design. Entry stairs lead up to the living areas, defined by arches and columns. A wall of built-ins and a fireplace highlight the contemporary great room, while four sets of French doors expand the living area to the wraparound porch. Second-floor sleeping quarters include a guest suite with a bayed sitting area, an additional bedroom and a full bath. The master suite features two walk-in closets, separate vanities and French doors to a private observation deck. The lower level offers bonus space for future use and another porch.

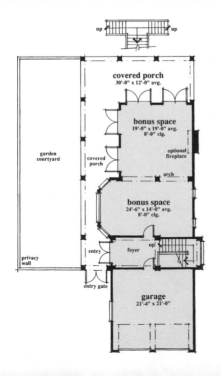

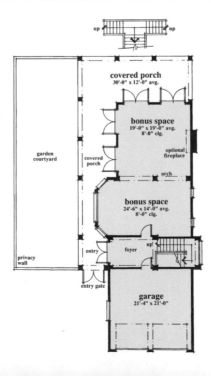

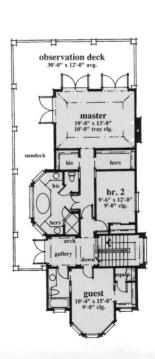

DESIGN
HPT890061

FIRST FLOOR: 874 SQ. FT.

SECOND FLOOR: 880 SQ. FT.

TOTAL: 1,754 SQ. FT.

FINISHED BASEMENT: 242 SQ. FT.

WIDTH: 34'-0"   DEPTH: 43'-0"

A STATELY TOWER adds a sense of grandeur to contemporary high-pitched rooflines on this dreamy Mediterranean-style villa. Surrounded by outdoor views, the living space extends to a veranda through three sets of French doors. Decorative columns announce the dining area, which boasts a ten-foot ceiling and views of its own. Tall arch-top windows bathe a winding staircase with sunlight or moonlight. The upper-level sleeping quarters include a master retreat that offers a bedroom with views and access to the observation deck. Secondary bedrooms share a full bath and linen storage. Bedroom 3 features a walk-in closet and French doors to the deck.

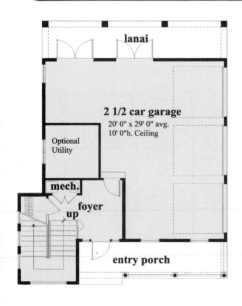

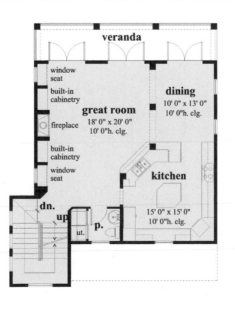

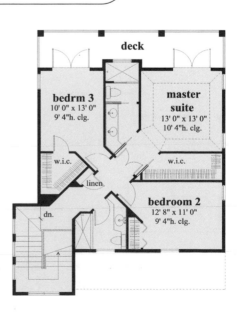

DESIGN
HPT890062

FIRST FLOOR: 1,383 SQ. FT.
SECOND FLOOR: 595 SQ. FT.
TOTAL: 1,978 SQ. FT.
BONUS SPACE: 617 SQ. FT.
WIDTH: 48'-0" DEPTH: 42'-0"

THE MIXTURE OF GRAND DETAILS with a comfortable layout makes this home a perfect combination of elegance and easy living. Those who prefer a spacious master suite set apart from the rest of the home will love this arrangement. The top story is devoted to a master suite with double doors leading to a private porch and a loft that overlooks the vaulted great room below. On the first floor, each of the two family bedrooms has an adjoining porch. The built-ins and fireplace in the great room give a feeling of casual sophistication.

DESIGN
HPT890063

FIRST FLOOR: 1,143 SQ. FT.
SECOND FLOOR: 651 SQ. FT.
TOTAL: 1,794 SQ. FT.
BONUS SPACE: 476 SQ. FT.
WIDTH: 32'-0" DEPTH: 57'-0"

ITALIAN COUNTRY ELEGANCE graces the exterior of this *casa bellisima*, swept in Mediterranean enchantment. The covered entryway extends into the foyer, where straight ahead, the two-story great room spaciously enhances the interior. This room features a warming fireplace and offers built-in cabinetry. The open dining room extends through double doors to the veranda on the left side on the plan. The adjacent kitchen features efficient pantry space. A family bedroom with a bath, a powder room and a utility room also reside on this main floor. Upstairs, a vaulted master suite with a vaulted private bath and deck share the floor with a loft area, which overlooks the great room. Downstairs, the basement-level bonus room and storage area share space with the two-car garage. Two lanais open on either side of the bonus room for additional outdoor patio space.

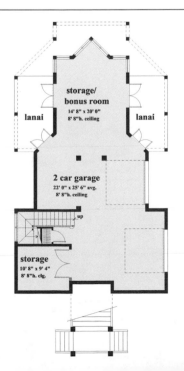

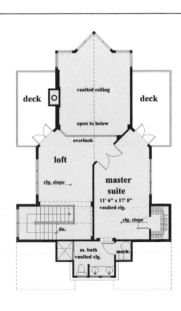

DESIGN
HPT890064

FIRST FLOOR: 1,828 SQ. FT.
SECOND FLOOR: 906 SQ. FT.
TOTAL: 2,734 SQ. FT.
WIDTH: 67'-4" DEPTH: 59'-8"

THIS UNIQUE contemporary/Floridian design brings all of the major living areas to the rear for extended outdoor livability. The separation of formal living areas adds excitement to dinner parties. A sunken living room leads to the covered patio. The sunken dining room shows unique detailing in its coffered ceiling. The large, efficient kitchen has a planning desk and is convenient to the dining room and a sunny breakfast room. A bayed den invites relaxation. Luxury abounds in the master suite, which includes a bath fit for royalty: two walk-in closets, dual vanities, a whirlpool tub and a shower. The second floor houses three more bedrooms—one with a sitting room—and two full baths.

DESIGN
HPT890065

FIRST FLOOR: 2,391 SQ. FT.
SECOND FLOOR: 922 SQ. FT.
TOTAL: 3,313 SQ. FT.
BONUS SPACE: 400 SQ. FT.
FINISHED BASEMENT: 1,964 SQ. FT.
WIDTH: 63'-10" DEPTH: 85'-6"

HERE'S AN UPSCALE MULTI-LEVEL PLAN with expansive rear views. The first floor provides an open living and dining area, defined by decorative columns and enhanced by natural light from tall windows. A breakfast area with a lovely triple window opens to a sun room, which allows light to pour into the gourmet kitchen. The master wing features a tray ceiling in the bedroom, two walk-in closets and an elegant private vestibule leading to a lavish bath. Upstairs, a reading loft overlooks the great room and leads to a sleeping area with two suites.

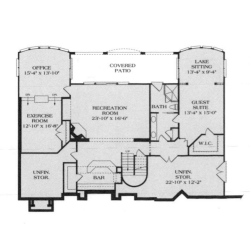

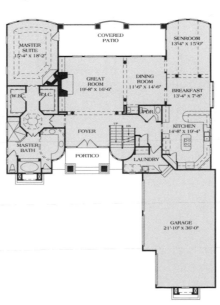

© The Sater Group, Inc.

DESIGN
HPT890066

FIRST FLOOR: 2,841 SQ. FT.
SECOND FLOOR: 1,052 SQ. FT.
TOTAL: 3,893 SQ. FT.
WIDTH: 85'-0" DEPTH: 76'-8"

ASSURE YOURSELF elegant living with this luxurious plan. A turret, two-story bay windows and plenty of arched glass impart a graceful style to the exterior, while rich amenities inside furnish contentment. A grand foyer decked with columns introduces the living room with a curve of glass windows viewing the rear gardens. A through-fireplace is shared by the study and living room. The master suite enjoys a tray ceiling, two walk-in closets, a separate shower and a garden tub set in a bay window. Informal entertainment will be a breeze with a rich leisure room adjoining the kitchen and breakfast nook and opening to a rear veranda. At the top of a lavish curving staircase are two family bedrooms sharing a full bath and a guest suite with a private deck.

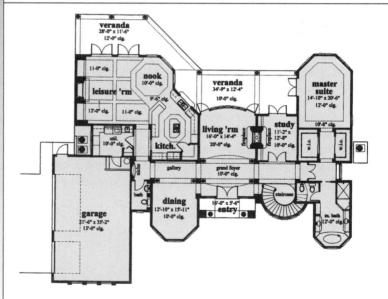

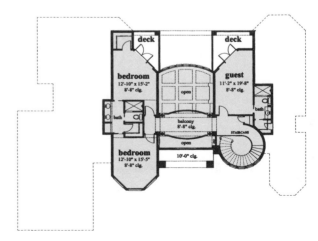

DESIGN
HPT890067

FIRST FLOOR: 2,285 SQ. FT.
SECOND FLOOR: 1,395 SQ. FT.
TOTAL: 3,680 SQ. FT.
BONUS SPACE: 300 SQ. FT.
WIDTH: 73'-8" DEPTH: 76'-2"

NOW HERE is a one-of-a-kind house plan. Step down from the raised foyer into the grand gallery where columns define the living room. This central living area boasts an enormous bow window with a fantastic view to the covered patio. The formal dining room is to the right and the lavish master suite sits on the left. The family gourmet will find an expansive kitchen beyond a pair of French doors on the right. The secluded family room completes this first level. An enormous den is found on the first landing above, to the left of the foyer. Two bedroom suites and a loft occupy the second floor.

DESIGN
HPT890068

FIRST FLOOR: 1,266 SQ. FT.
SECOND FLOOR: 1,324 SQ. FT.
TOTAL: 2,590 SQ. FT.
WIDTH: 34'-0"   DEPTH: 63'-2"

THIS FLORIDIAN-STYLE HOME BOASTS an impressive balcony that is sure to catch the eye. A large veranda borders two sides of the home. The entry leads into a long foyer, which runs from the entrance to the rear of the design. The coffered great room enjoys a fireplace, built-in cabinetry and French doors to the veranda; the dining room also accesses the veranda. The island kitchen leads into a bayed nook, perfect for Sunday morning breakfasting. The second floor is home to two family bedrooms, both with access to the deck, a study and a luxurious master suite. A vaulted sitting area, full bath and deck access are just some of the highlights of the master suite.

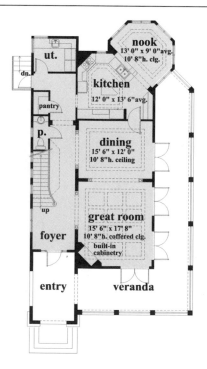

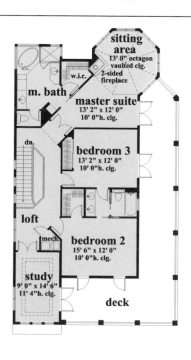

DESIGN
HPT890069

FIRST FLOOR: 1,642 SQ. FT.
SECOND FLOOR: 1,165 SQ. FT.
TOTAL: 2,807 SQ. FT.
LOWER FOYER: 150 SQ. FT.
WIDTH: 44'-6"   DEPTH: 58'-0"

HURRICANE SHUTTERS LET FRESH AIR IN, while five decks make the outside easily accessible. Inside, the open living and dining area is defined by two pairs of French doors that frame a two-story wall of glass, while built-ins flank the living room fireplace. The efficient kitchen features a walk-in pantry, a work island and a door to the covered porch. Split sleeping quarters offer privacy to the first-floor master suite. Upstairs, a gallery loft leads to a computer area with a built-in desk and a balcony overlook. This home is designed with a pier foundation.

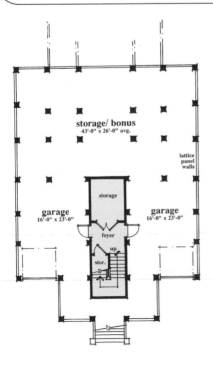

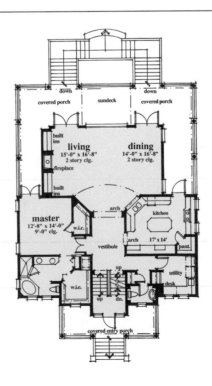

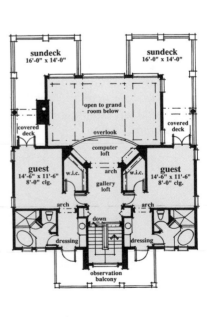

DESIGN
HPT890070

SQUARE FOOTAGE: 2,662 SQ. FT.
FINISHED BASEMENT 1,548 SQ. FT.
WIDTH: 98'-0" DEPTH: 64'-8" [L][D]

HERE'S A HILLSIDE HAVEN for family living with plenty of room to entertain in style. Enter the main level from a dramatic columned portico that leads to a large entry hall. The gathering room, graced by a fireplace and sliding glass doors to the rear deck, is straight back and adjoins a formal dining area. A true gourmet kitchen with plenty of room for casual eating and conversation is nearby. The abundantly appointed master suite on this level is complemented by a luxurious bath complete with His and Hers walk-in closets, a whirlpool tub in a bumped-out bay and a separate shower. On the lower level are two more bedrooms—each with access to the rear terrace, a full bath, a large activity area with a fireplace and a convenient summer kitchen.

© 1999 Donald A. Gardner Architects, Inc.

DESIGN
HPT890071

FIRST FLOOR: 1,170 SQ. FT.
SECOND FLOOR: 1,058 SQ. FT.
TOTAL: 2,228 SQ. FT.
WIDTH: 30'-0" DEPTH: 51'-0"

AN ELEVATED PIER FOUNDATION, narrow width, and front and rear porches make this home perfect for waterfront lots, while its squared-off design makes it easy to afford. The great room, kitchen and breakfast area are all open for a casual and spacious feeling. Numerous windows enhance the area's volume. Flexible rooms located at the front of the home include a formal living or dining room and a study or bedroom with optional entry to the powder room. Upstairs, every bedroom (plus the master bath) enjoys porch access. The master suite features a tray ceiling, dual closets and a sizable bath with linen cabinets.

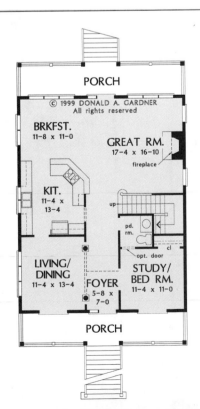

DESIGN
HPT890072

FIRST FLOOR: 1,073 SQ. FT.
SECOND FLOOR: 470 SQ. FT.
TOTAL: 1,543 SQ. FT.
WIDTH: 30'-0" DEPTH: 71'-6"

HOLDING THE NARROWEST of foot-prints, this adorable little seaside plan is big on interior space—perfect for low-lying beachfront areas. The family room has three big windows and opens to the tiled U-shaped kitchen and breakfast nook, with access to the rear deck. The master bed-room, which includes a walk-in closet, and another bedroom share a full bath on this floor. Two more bedrooms and another bath are upstairs. A convenient utility room is located on the main level.

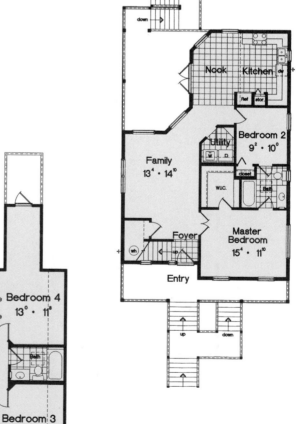

DESIGN
HPT890073

FIRST FLOOR: 1,366 SQ. FT.
SECOND FLOOR: 689 SQ. FT.
TOTAL: 2,055 SQ. FT.
WIDTH: 49'-4" DEPTH: 50'-4"

WITH AN ELEVATED PIER foundation, this stunning home is perfect for waterfront properties. Magnificent porches, a balcony and a plethora of picture windows take advantage of the beach or lakeside views. The great room features a ten-foot beam ceiling, a fireplace and a space-saving built-in entertainment center. The staircase is highlighted by a grand window with an arched top, while a Palladian window accents the upstairs loft/study. The master bedroom is the essence of luxury with skylights, a fireplace, cathedral ceiling, balcony, vaulted bath and oversized walk-in closet. Family bedrooms on the first floor share a full bath. Note the front and rear wrapping porches.

© 1998 Donald A Gardner Architects, Inc.

©1998 Donald A. Gardner, Inc.

DESIGN
HPT890074

FIRST FLOOR: 944 SQ. FT.
SECOND FLOOR: 826 SQ. FT.
TOTAL: 1,770 SQ. FT.
WIDTH: 30'-4" DEPTH: 42'-8"

THIS WATERFRONT HOME FEATURES a super-slim design for very narrow lots, but plenty of room for family and friends. A two-story ceiling amplifies the open great room with its overlooking second-floor balcony and clerestory windows. The master suite enjoys views from its second-floor porch while pampering homeowners with a large walk-in closet and a bath with His and Hers vanities separated by a garden tub. Two secondary bedrooms and two full baths complete this home's comfortable design.

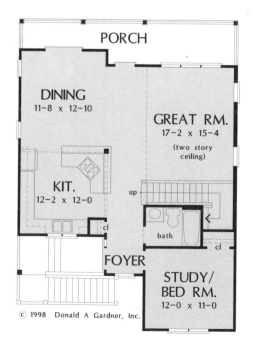

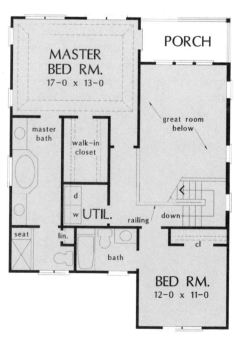

80

DESIGN
HPT890075

FIRST FLOOR: 907 SQ. FT.
SECOND FLOOR: 872 SQ. FT.
TOTAL: 1,779 SQ. FT.
WIDTH: 34'-0" DEPTH: 30'-0"

TWO STORIES and still up on a pier foundation! A covered front porch leads to two sets of French doors—one to the spacious living room and one to the dining area. An L-shaped kitchen features a work island, a nearby utility room and plenty of counter and cabinet space. A sun room finishes off this floor with class. Upstairs, the sleeping zone consists of two family bedrooms—one with access to a balcony—a full bath and a master suite. Here, the homeowner will surely be pleased with a walk-in closet, a corner tub and a separate shower, as well as balcony access.

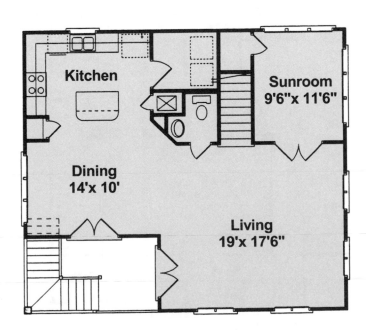

Kitchen

Sunroom
9'6"x 11'6"

Dining
14'x 10'

Living
19'x 17'6"

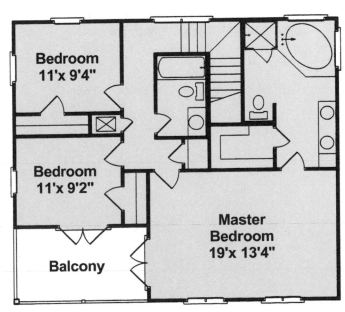

Bedroom
11'x 9'4"

Bedroom
11'x 9'2"

Balcony

Master
Bedroom
19'x 13'4"

DESIGN
HPT890076

FIRST FLOOR: 965 SQ. FT.
SECOND FLOOR: 739 SQ. FT.
TOTAL: 1,704 SQ. FT.
WIDTH: 41'-4" DEPTH: 30'-10"

WITH ITS ELEVATED PIER foundation, this home is well suited to coastal locations. Principal rooms are oriented toward the rear of the home for premium waterfront views. On the first floor, a two-story ceiling adds drama and space to the great room, which is open to the dining room and kitchen for a large gathering area. The great room, dining room and study/bedroom all open to the rear porch. Upstairs, a balcony overlooking the great room and foyer joins the master suite and a secondary bedroom and bath.

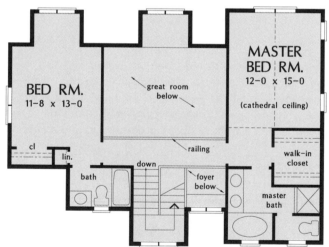

BED RM.
11-8 x 13-0

cl
lin.
bath
down
great room below
railing
foyer below

MASTER BED RM.
12-0 x 15-0
(cathedral ceiling)

walk-in closet
master bath

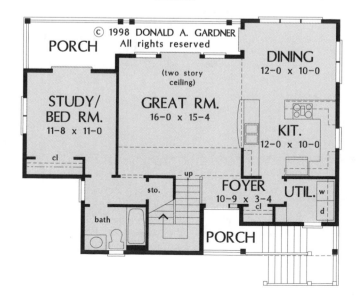

PORCH

© 1998 DONALD A. GARDNER
All rights reserved

DINING
12-0 x 10-0

STUDY/ BED RM.
11-8 x 11-0

(two story ceiling)

GREAT RM.
16-0 x 15-4

KIT.
12-0 x 10-0

cl
sto.
up
bath

FOYER
10-9 x 3-4

UTIL.
w
d
cl

PORCH

DESIGN
HPT890077

FIRST FLOOR: 912 SQ. FT.
SECOND FLOOR: 831 SQ. FT.
TOTAL: 1,743 SQ. FT.
WIDTH: 34'-0" DEPTH: 32'-0"

WITH A PIER FOUNDATION, this two-story home is perfect for an oceanfront lot. The main level consists of an open living area that flows into the dining area adjacent to the kitchen. Here, a walk-in pantry and plenty of counter and cabinet space will please the gourmet of the family. A full bath and a utility room complete this floor. Upstairs, the sleeping zone is complete with two family bedrooms sharing a linen closet and a full hall bath, as well as a deluxe master bedroom. Features here include a private balcony, a walk-in closet and a dual-vanity bath.

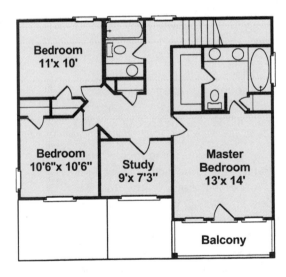

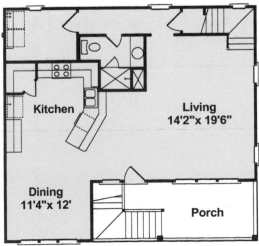

DESIGN
HPT890078

FIRST FLOOR: 1,212 SQ. FT.
SECOND FLOOR: 620 SQ. FT.
TOTAL: 1,832 SQ. FT.
WIDTH: 38'-0" DEPTH: 40'-0"

THIS COMFORTABLE VACATION design provides two levels of relaxing family space. The main level offers a spacious wrapping front porch and an abundance of windows, filling interior spaces with the summer sunshine. A two-sided fireplace warms the living room/dining room combination and a master bedroom that features a roomy walk-in closet. Nearby, the hall bath offers a relaxing whirlpool tub. The kitchen is open and features an island snack bar and pantry storage. A cozy sun room accesses the wrapping deck. Upstairs, two additional bedrooms feature ample closet space and share a second-floor bath. This home is designed with a basement foundation.

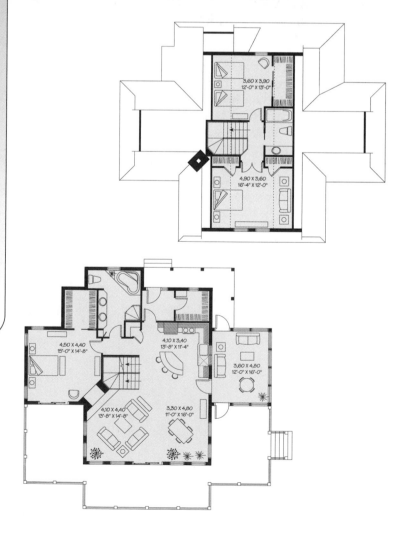

DESIGN
HPT890079

FIRST FLOOR: 1,182 SQ. FT.
SECOND FLOOR: 838 SQ. FT.
TOTAL: 2,020 SQ. FT.
WIDTH: 34'-0" DEPTH: 52'-0"

THIS TWO-STORY COASTAL HOME finds its inspiration in a Craftsman style that's highlighted by ornamented gables. Open planning is the key with the living and dining areas sharing the front of the first floor with the U-shaped kitchen and stairway. Both the dining room and the living room access the second porch. The master suite boasts a walk-in closet, private vanity and angled tub. The utility room is efficiently placed between the kitchen and bath. Bedrooms 2 and 3 share a bath while Bedroom 4 enjoys a private bath.

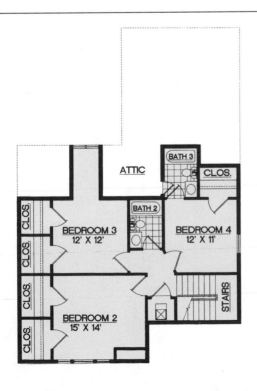

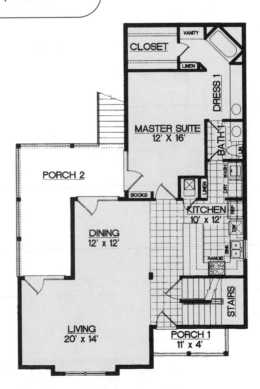

DESIGN
HPT890080

FIRST FLOOR: 895 SQ. FT.
SECOND FLOOR: 576 SQ. FT.
TOTAL: 1,471 SQ. FT.
WIDTH: 26'-0" DEPTH: 36'-0"

HERE'S A FAVORITE WATERFRONT HOME with plenty of space to kick back and relax. A lovely sun room opens from the dining room and allows great views. An angled hearth warms the living and dining areas. Three lovely windows brighten the dining space, which leads out to a stunning sun porch. The gourmet kitchen has an island counter with a snack bar. The first-floor master bedroom enjoys a walk-in closet and a nearby bath. Upstairs, a spacious bath with a whirlpool tub is thoughtfully placed between two bedrooms. A daylight basement allows a lower-level portico. This home is designed with a basement foundation.

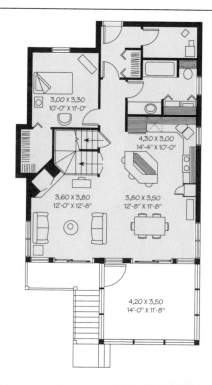

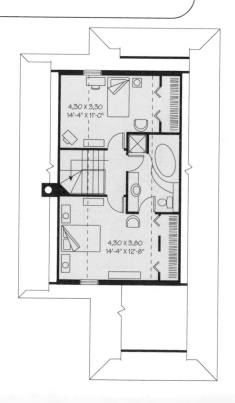

DESIGN
HPT890081

FIRST FLOOR: 895 SQ. FT.
SECOND FLOOR: 576 SQ. FT.
TOTAL: 1,471 SQ. FT.
WIDTH: 26'-0" DEPTH: 36'-0"

THIS VACATION HOME enjoys a screened porch and sits on stilts to avoid any water damage. Truly a free-flowing plan, the dining room, living room and kitchen share a common space, with no walls separating them. An island snack counter in the kitchen provides plenty of space for food preparation. A family bedroom and full bath complete the first level. Upstairs, two additional bedrooms—with ample closet space—share a lavish bath, which includes a whirlpool tub and separate shower. This home is designed with a basement foundation.

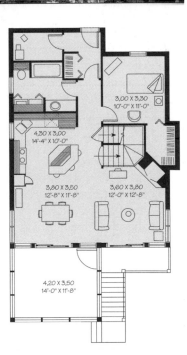

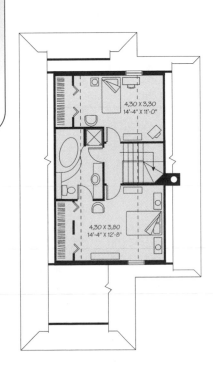

DESIGN
HPT890082

SQUARE FOOTAGE: 2,136
BONUS SPACE: 1,428 SQ. FT.
WIDTH: 44'-0"   DEPTH: 63'-0"

THIS RAISED TIDEWATER design is well suited for many building situations, with comfortable outdoor areas that encourage year-round living. Horizontal siding and a steeply pitched roof call up a sense of the past, while a smart-space interior redefines the luxury of comfort with up-to-the-minute amenities. A vaulted ceiling highlights the great room, made comfy by a centered fireplace, extensive built-ins and French doors that let in fresh air and sunlight. The formal dining room opens from the entry hall and features a triple-window view of the side property. A secluded sitting area in the master suite features a wide window and a door to a private area of the rear porch. Two secondary bedrooms share a full bath.

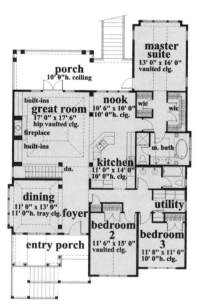

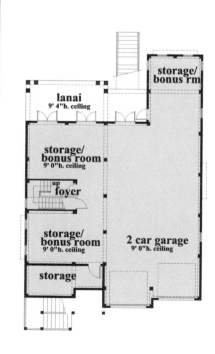

© 1998 Donald A Gardner, Inc.

L.B. NATHAN

DESIGN
HPT890083

FIRST FLOOR: 1,650 SQ. FT.
SECOND FLOOR: 712 SQ. FT.
TOTAL: 2,362 SQ. FT.
WIDTH: 58'-10" DEPTH: 47'-4"

CEDAR SHAKES and striking gables with decorative scalloped insets adorn the exterior of this lovely coastal home. The generous great room is expanded by a rear wall of windows, with additional light from transom windows above the front door and a rear clerestory dormer. The kitchen features a pass-through to the great room. The dining room, great room and study all access an inviting back porch. The master bedroom is a treat with a private balcony, His and Hers walk-in closets and an impeccable bath. Upstairs, a room-sized loft with an arched opening overlooks the great room below. Two more bedrooms, one with its own private balcony, share a hall bath.

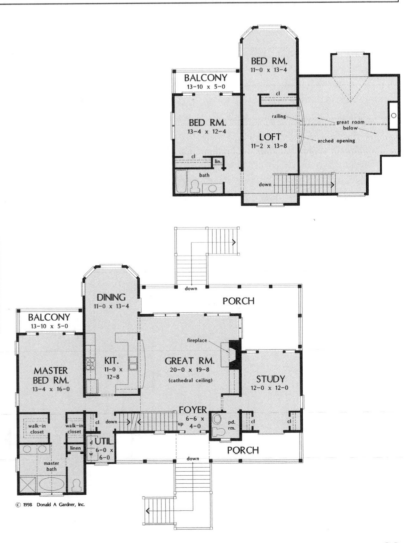

© 1998 Donald A Gardner, Inc.

DESIGN
HPT890084

FIRST FLOOR: 1,537 SQ. FT.
SECOND FLOOR: 812 SQ. FT.
TOTAL: 2,349 SQ. FT.
BONUS SPACE: 581 SQ. FT.
WIDTH: 45'-4" DEPTH: 50'-0"

DRAMATIC ROOFLINES cap a host of asymmetrical gables and complement a variety of windows on this visually stunning coastal cottage. A mid-level foyer leads up to the main-level great room, which opens to the rear porch through grand French doors, providing views and easing the transition to the outside space. In the heart of the home, the gourmet kitchen serves a stunning formal dining room. To the left of the plan, a secluded master suite boasts a coffered ceiling, walk-in closet and private access to one of the rear porches. A grand central staircase leads to the upper-level sleeping quarters and offers a splendid window that brings sunlight indoors. Generous sitting space at the head of the stairs can convert to a computer loft.

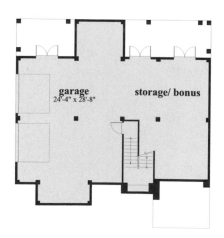

garage
24'-4" x 28'-8"

storage/ bonus

porch
13'-4" x 8'-6"
9'-4" clg.

dining
11'-0" x 11'-0"
9'-4" clg.

porch
20'-0" x 8'-6"
9'-4" clg.

master
13'-0" x 18'-0"
vaulted

kitch.
11'-0" x
13'-0"

great 'rm
17'-4" x 18'-0"
vaulted

fireplace

w.i.c.

util.

m. bath

porch
13'-0" x 11'-0"

bedroom
11'-0" x 13'-0"
9'-4" clg.

crow's nest
12'-6" x 14'-2"
9'-4" clg.

bath

open

loft
7'-6" x
11'-10"
8' clg.

bedroom
12'-2" x 12'-10"
9'-4" clg.

DESIGN
HPT890085

FIRST FLOOR: 1,671 SQ. FT.
SECOND FLOOR: 846 SQ. FT.
TOTAL: 2,517 SQ. FT.
LOWER FOYER: 140 SQ. FT.
WIDTH: 44'-0" DEPTH: 55'-0"

EXOTIC TROPICAL BREEZES will find their way through the joyful rooms of this just-right cottage, bringing with them a sense of tranquillity and contentment. The great room provides such luxurious amenities as a vaulted ceiling, built-ins, a grand fireplace and an overlook from the upper-level gallery hall. An efficient island kitchen is nestled between a sunny nook and the formal dining room, which is elegantly defined by regal columns. Pocket doors open to a private study to the left of the foyer. Secondary sleeping quarters on this level include two family bedrooms that share a full bath, with a laundry conveniently placed nearby. The upper level is dedicated to the expansive master suite, which boasts a private veranda, tray ceiling, sitting room and walk-in closet. The lower level provides a three-car garage, a lanai and a bonus room.

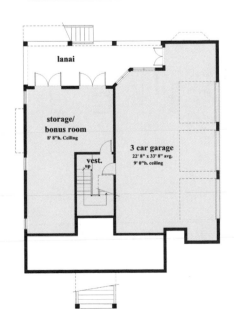

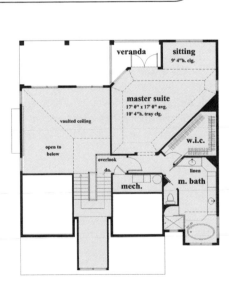

DESIGN
HPT890086

FIRST FLOOR: 1,342 SQ. FT.
SECOND FLOOR: 511 SQ. FT.
TOTAL: 1,853 SQ. FT.
WIDTH: 44'-0" DEPTH: 40'-0"

DETAILED FRETWORK complements a standing-seam roof on this tropical cottage. An arch-top transom provides an absolutely perfect highlight to the classic clapboard facade. An unrestrained floor plan offers cool digs for kicking back, and a sensational retreat for guests—whether the occasion is formal or casual. French doors open to a rear porch from the great room letting in fresh air and the sights and sounds of the great outdoors. Inside, the master bedroom leads to a dressing space with linen storage and a walk-in closet. The lavish bath includes a garden tub, oversized shower and a wraparound vanity with two lavatories. Two secondary bedrooms on the upper level share a spacious loft that overlooks the great room. One of the bedrooms opens to a private deck.

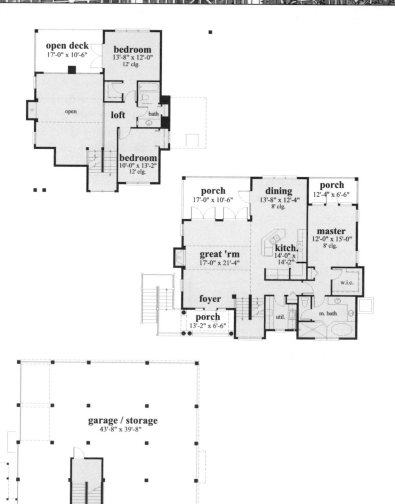

open deck
17'-0" x 10'-6"

bedroom
13'-8" x 12'-0"
12' clg.

open

loft

bath

bedroom
10'-0" x 13'-2"
12' clg.

porch
17'-0" x 10'-6"

dining
13'-8" x 12'-4"
8' clg.

porch
12'-4" x 6'-6"

master
12'-0" x 15'-0"
8' clg.

great 'rm
17'-0" x 21'-4"

kitch.
14'-0" x
14'-2"

w.i.c.

foyer

util.

m. bath

porch
13'-2" x 6'-6"

garage / storage
43'-8" x 39'-8"

DESIGN
HPT890087

FIRST FLOOR: 1,383 SQ. FT.
SECOND FLOOR: 595 SQ. FT.
TOTAL: 1,978 SQ. FT.
BONUS SPACE: 617 SQ. FT.
WIDTH: 48'-0" DEPTH: 42'-0"

THIS FABULOUS KEY WEST HOME blends interior space with the great outdoors. Designed for a balmy climate, this home boasts expansive porches and decks—with outside access from every area of the home. A sun-dappled foyer leads via a stately mid-level staircase to a splendid great room, which features a warming fireplace tucked in beside beautiful built-in cabinetry. Highlighted by a wall of glass that opens to the rear porch, this two-story living space opens to the formal dining room and a well-appointed kitchen. Spacious secondary bedrooms on the main level open to outside spaces and share a full bath. Upstairs, a ten-foot tray ceiling highlights a private master suite, which provides French doors to an upper-level porch.

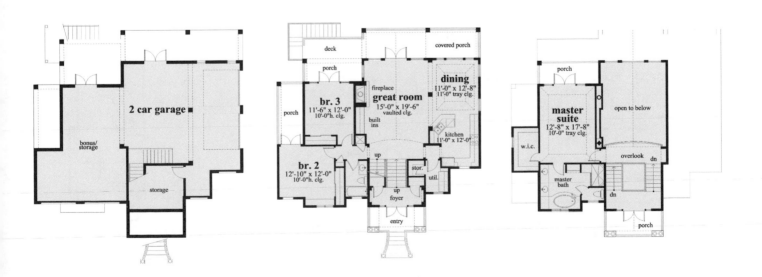

DESIGN
HPT890088

FIRST FLOOR: 1,586 SQ. FT.
SECOND FLOOR: 601 SQ. FT.
TOTAL: 2,187 SQ. FT.
WIDTH: 50'-0" DEPTH: 44'-0"

LATTICE WALLS, PICKETS AND HORIZONTAL SIDING COMPLEMENT a relaxed Key West design that's perfect for waterfront properties. The grand room with a fireplace, the dining room and Bedroom 2 open through French doors to the veranda. The master suite occupies the entire second floor and features access to a private balcony through double doors. This pampering suite also includes a spacious walk-in closet and a full bath with a whirlpool tub. Enclosed storage/bonus space and a garage are available on the lower level. This home is designed with a pier foundation.

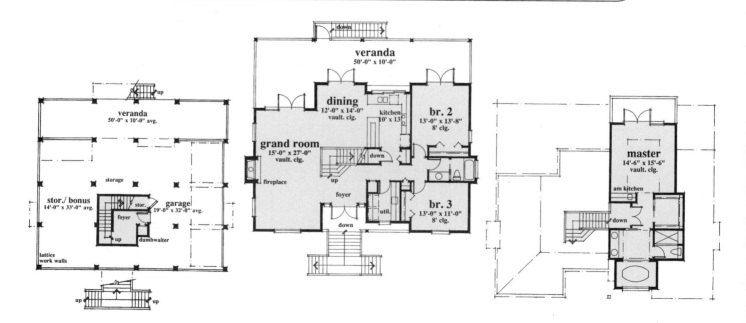

DESIGN
HPT890089

MAIN LEVEL: 2,061 SQ. FT.
SECOND LEVEL: 464 SQ. FT.
TOTAL: 2,525 SQ. FT.
FINISHED BASEMENT: 452 SQ. FT.
WIDTH: 50'-0" DEPTH: 63'-0"

THIS WATERFRONT HOME offers classic seaboard details with louvered shutters, covered porches and an open floor plan. The lower level is comprised of two single-car garages, a game room with an accompanying full bath and a utility room. The U-shaped staircase leads to the main living areas where the island kitchen is open to the dining room. The living room offers a wall of windows with access to the rear porch and deck. Two bedrooms lie to the left and share a full bath. On the right are the master suite and a fourth bedroom—each with a private bath. Upstairs, a fifth bedroom with a bath completes the plan.

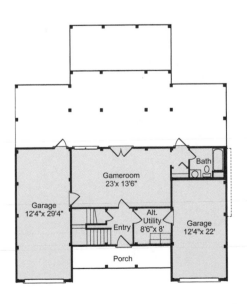

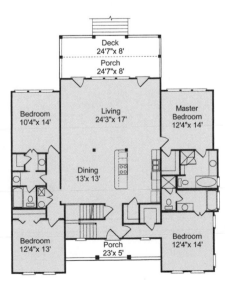

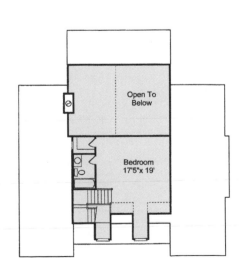

DESIGN
HPT890090

FIRST FLOOR: 1,855 SQ. FT.
SECOND FLOOR: 901 SQ. FT.
TOTAL: 2,756 SQ. FT.
WIDTH: 66'-0" DEPTH: 50'-0"

THIS SOUTHERN TIDEWATER cottage is the perfect vacation hideaway. An octagonal great room with a multi-faceted vaulted ceiling illuminates the interior. The island kitchen is brightened by a bumped-out window and a pass-through to the lanai. Two walk-in closets and a whirlpool bath await to indulge the homeowner in the master suite. A set of double doors opens to the vaulted master lanai for quiet comfort. The U-shaped staircase leads to a loft, which overlooks the great room and the foyer. Two additional family bedrooms are offered with private baths. A computer center and a morning kitchen complete the upstairs.

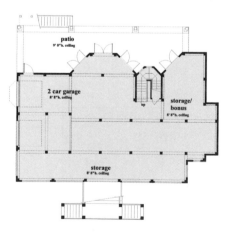

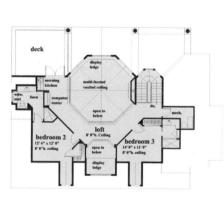

DESIGN
HPT890091

FIRST FLOOR: 2,390 SQ. FT.
SECOND FLOOR: 1,200 SQ. FT.
TOTAL: 3,590 SQ. FT.
WIDTH: 61'-0"   DEPTH: 64'-4"

THIS LUXURIOUS WATERFRONT design sings of Southern island influences. A front covered porch opens to a foyer, flanked by a study and dining room. The living room, warmed by a fireplace and safe from off-season ocean breezes, overlooks the rear covered porch. The island kitchen extends into a breakfast room. Beyond the covered porch, the wood deck is also accessed privately from the master suite. This suite includes a private whirlpool bath and huge walk-in closet. A guest suite is located on the first floor, while two additional bedrooms and a multimedia room are located on the second level.

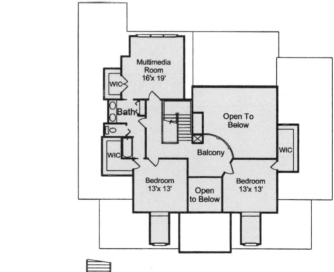

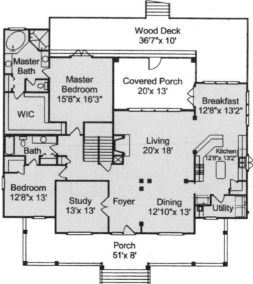

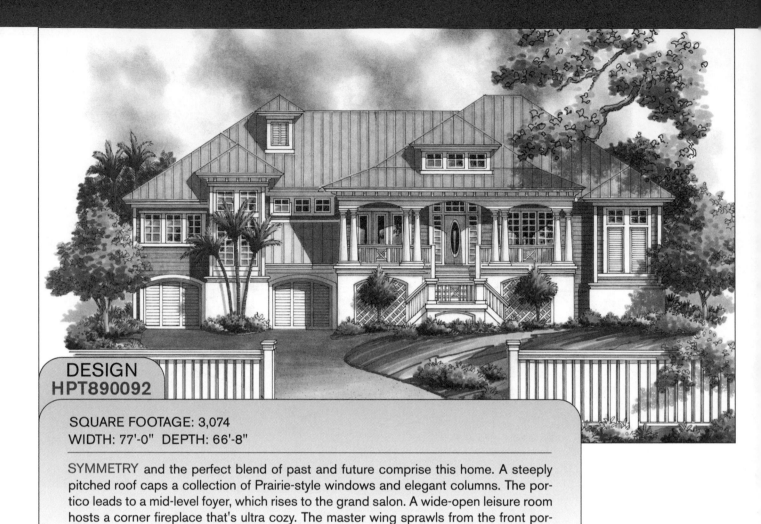

DESIGN
HPT890092

SQUARE FOOTAGE: 3,074
WIDTH: 77'-0" DEPTH: 66'-8"

SYMMETRY and the perfect blend of past and future comprise this home. A steeply pitched roof caps a collection of Prairie-style windows and elegant columns. The portico leads to a mid-level foyer, which rises to the grand salon. A wide-open leisure room hosts a corner fireplace that's ultra cozy. The master wing sprawls from the front portico to the rear covered porch, rich with luxury amenities and plenty of secluded space.

Lower Porch

2 Car Garage / Storage

Guest Suite
15'-0"x11'-0"

Leisure Room
17'-6"x19'-3"

Porch
68'-0"x15'-3"

Nook

Guest Suite
10'-10"x13'-0"

Kitchen
16'-8"x14'-8"

Wet Bar

Grand Salon
17'-4"x18'-6"

Powder Bath

Master Retreat
15'-1"x20'-0"

WIC

Utility
10'-10"x6'-6"

WIC

A/C Comp

Dining Room
12'-0"x16'-0"

Foyer

Study
11'-3"x15'-2"

Master Bath

Porch

Portico

DESIGN
HPT890093

FIRST FLOOR: 2,350 SQ. FT.
SECOND FLOOR: 1,338 SQ. FT.
TOTAL: 3,688 SQ. FT.
FINISHED BASEMENT: 1,509 SQ. FT.
WIDTH: 63'-0" DEPTH: 72'-10"

GET AWAY TO THIS ISLAND OF LUXURY—two or three family bedrooms and one enormous master suite should provide plenty of room for the entire crew. Enter the foyer via French doors to gain easy access to all levels. The basement level accesses a covered patio and allows future space for a summer kitchen, game room, home office, media room and a guest suite with an adjacent bath. Entertaining will be easy with the gathering room, dining area and Florida room that are open to one another and adjoin the rear covered patio. The master suite and a hobby room occupy the second level. An enormous walk-in closet, sumptuous bath and roomy private deck enhance the master bedroom.

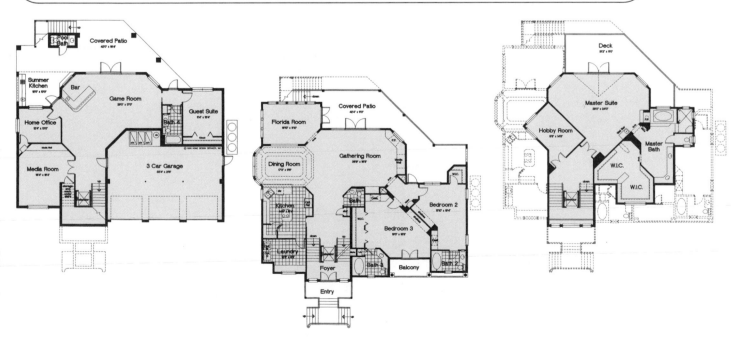

DESIGN
HPT890094

FIRST FLOOR: 507 SQ. FT.
SECOND FLOOR: 495 SQ. FT.
TOTAL: 1,002 SQ. FT.
WIDTH: 20'-4" DEPTH: 24'-4"

SIMPLE FARMHOUSE style includes a wrapping porch, accessible at the front and the back of this home. The living area, dining area and kitchen are open to one another and share space on the first floor with a full bath and large hall closet. Bedrooms are on the second level and include one with balcony access. Choose this design as a primary residence or as a charming lakeside retreat. This home is designed with a basement foundation.

2,40 X 3,30
8'-0" X 11'-0"

3,00 X 3,00
10'-0" X 10'-0"

3,60 X 3,60
12'-0" X 12'-0"

3,60 X 3,30
12'-0" X 11'-0"

4,50 X 3,60
15'-0" X 12'-0"

DESIGN
HPT890095

FIRST FLOOR: 871 SQ. FT.
SECOND FLOOR: 1,047 SQ. FT.
TOTAL: 1,918 SQ. FT.
WIDTH: 32'-0" DEPTH: 47'-0"

WITH ITS SHINGLE and siding exterior, this home has an air of oceanfront living. A large covered porch accesses a spacious gathering room, complete with a fireplace and optional shelving units. An archway leads from the gathering room to the dining room, which is highlighted with a wall of windows and boasts a doorway to the kitchen. The breakfast area overlooks a screened porch and flows smoothly into a U-shaped kitchen. The sleeping quarters reside upstairs and include two family suites, two full baths, a master suite with a tray ceiling, and a convenient laundry room.

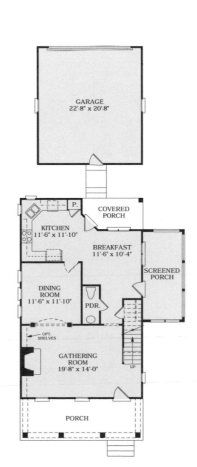

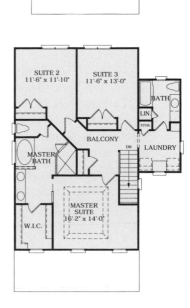

DESIGN
HPT890096

FIRST FLOOR: 2,193 SQ. FT.
SECOND FLOOR: 1,136 SQ. FT.
TOTAL: 3,329 SQ. FT.
FUTURE GAME ROOM: 347 SQ. FT.
WIDTH: 41'-6" DEPTH: 71'-4"

THIS FARMHOUSE is far from old-fashioned with a computer loft/library and future game room designed into the second floor. Two wrapping porches grace the exterior, offering expanded outdoor living spaces. The breakfast nook, dining room and family room radiate off the central island kitchen. The study/bedroom at the front is situated with an adjacent full bath, making this ideal for a guest room. Three bedrooms share two baths on the second floor while the master suite, with its elaborate private bath, finds seclusion on the first floor.

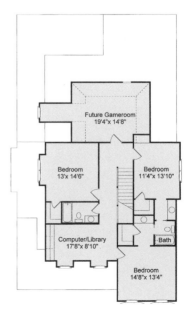

DESIGN
HPT890097

FIRST FLOOR: 1,376 SQ. FT.
SECOND FLOOR: 695 SQ. FT.
TOTAL: 2,071 SQ. FT.
BONUS SPACE: 723 SQ. FT.
WIDTH: 47'-0" DEPTH: 49'-8"

THE UNIQUE CHARM of this farmhouse begins with a flight of steps and a welcoming, covered front porch. Just inside, the foyer leads to the formal dining room on the left—with easy access to the kitchen—and straight ahead to the great room. Here, a fireplace and built-in entertainment center are balanced by access to the rear screened porch. The first-floor master suite provides plenty of privacy, while upstairs two family bedrooms share a full bath. The lower level offers space for a fourth bedroom, a recreation room and a garage.

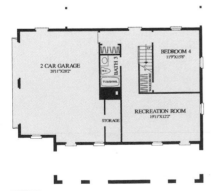

DESIGN
HPT890098

FIRST FLOOR: 1,362 SQ. FT.
SECOND FLOOR: 481 SQ. FT.
TOTAL: 1,843 SQ. FT.
WIDTH: 49'-4" DEPTH: 44'-10"

AN ENCHANTING WRAPAROUND porch, delightful dormers and bright bay windows create excitement inside and out for this coastal home. The large center dormer brightens the vaulted foyer, while the great room enjoys added light from a trio of rear clerestory windows. A balcony dividing the second-floor bedrooms overlooks the great room and visually connects the two floors. The master suite is located on the first floor and features back-porch access, a walk-in closet and a private bath with a garden tub and separate shower. The second-floor bedrooms, each with a dormer alcove, share a hall bath that includes a dual-sink vanity.

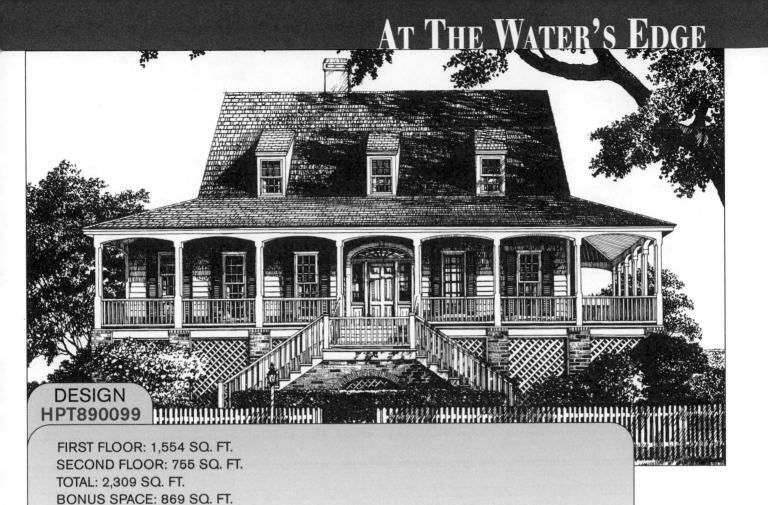

DESIGN
HPT890099

FIRST FLOOR: 1,554 SQ. FT.
SECOND FLOOR: 755 SQ. FT.
TOTAL: 2,309 SQ. FT.
BONUS SPACE: 869 SQ. FT.
WIDTH: 57'-6" DEPTH: 39'-6"

A GRACEFUL SET OF STEPS lead to an impressive wraparound porch, encouraging lemonade afternoons and evening stargazing. Inside, the foyer introduces the formal dining room to the left and the great room just ahead—complete with a fireplace, built-ins and rear-deck access. The U-shaped kitchen features a pantry, built-in planning desk and an adjacent breakfast area. Located on the first-floor for privacy, the master suite offers a large walk-in closet and a lavish bath with a separate tub and shower. Upstairs, two spacious bedrooms share a full bath with an interesting sink area. The basement level is complete with a fourth bedroom, full bath and a recreation room.

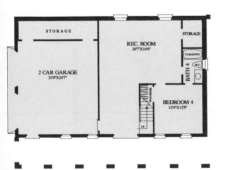

DESIGN
HPT890100

SQUARE FOOTAGE: 840
WIDTH: 33'-0" DEPTH: 31'-0"

THIS CHARMING HOME is ideal for waterfront property with a generous wrap-around porch The porch features a corner gazebo that's perfect for outdoor living. The vestibule offers an energy- and space-efficient pocket door that opens to the island kitchen and dining room where sliding glass doors open to the gazebo. The living room views in three directions, bringing the outside in. A bedroom and lavish bath complete the floor plan. This home is designed with a basement foundation.

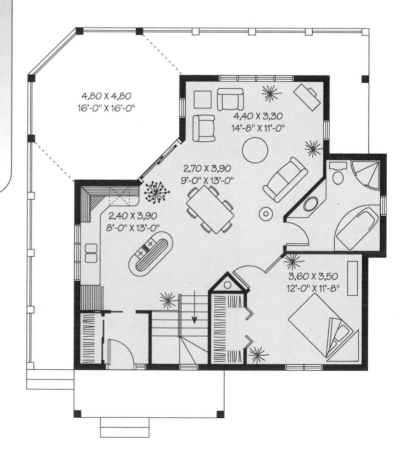

DESIGN
HPT890101

SQUARE FOOTAGE: 1,520
WIDTH: 40'-0" DEPTH: 59'-0"

SIZE DOESN'T ALWAYS predict amenities! This one-story pier-foundation home is only 1,520 square feet, but it's packed with surprises. The spacious living room offers a huge wall of windows to show off the beach, while a fireplace offers warmth on cool winter evenings. The L-shaped kitchen features an angled work island and easily accesses the adjacent dining area. Three secondary bedrooms share a full bath and provide ample room for family or guests. The master bedroom is complete with a walk-in closet and a private bath. Please specify crawlspace or pier foundation when ordering.

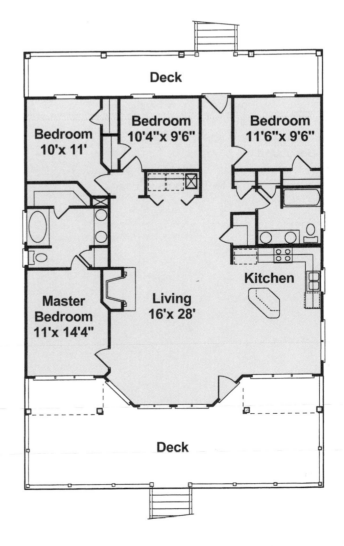

DESIGN
HPT890102

SQUARE FOOTAGE: 1,649
WIDTH: 72'-0" DEPTH: 54'-6"

THE GRAND ENTRY of this three-bedroom home is just the start its appeal. The wraparound porch offers plenty of room for stargazing or enjoying ocean breezes. Inside, a spacious living room is highlighted by angled windows and a warming fireplace. The adjacent kitchen and dining area gives this space an open, welcoming feeling. Separated for privacy, two family bedrooms share a bath on the right side of the home, while the master bedroom is located to the left of the plan.

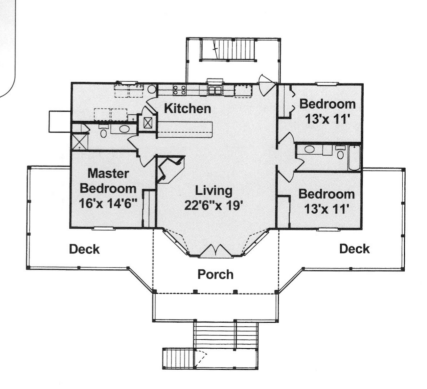

DESIGN
HPT890103

SQUARE FOOTAGE: 1,578
WIDTH: 83'-0" DEPTH: 40'-6"

WITH A GRACEFUL PEDIMENT above and a sturdy, columned veranda below, this quaint home was made for country living. The veranda wraps slightly around on two sides of the facade and permits access to a central foyer with a den (or third bedroom) on the right and the country kitchen on the left. Look for an island work space in the kitchen and a plant ledge over the entry between the great room and the kitchen. A fireplace warms the great room and is flanked by windows overlooking the rear deck. A casually defined dining space has double-door access to this same deck.

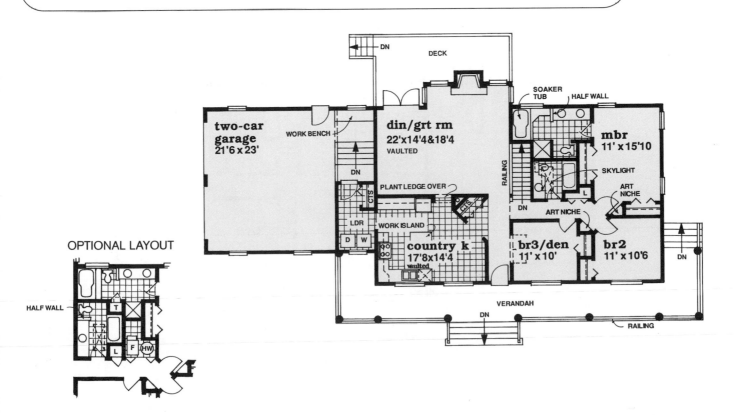

OPTIONAL LAYOUT

HALF WALL

two-car garage 21'6 x 23'

WORK BENCH

DN

DN

DECK

SOAKER TUB   HALF WALL

din/grt rm 22'x14'4 & 18'4
VAULTED

RAILING

mbr 11' x 15'10

SKYLIGHT

PLANT LEDGE OVER

DN

ART NICHE

LDR

WORK ISLAND

ART NICHE

D W

country k 17'8 x14'4
vaulted

br3/den 11' x 10'

br2 11' x 10'6

DN

VERANDAH

DN

RAILING

DESIGN
HPT890104

SQUARE FOOTAGE: 1,408
WIDTH: 70'-0" DEPTH: 34'-0"

AN EYEBROW DORMER and a large veranda give guests a warm country greeting outside, while inside vaulted ceilings lend a sense of spaciousness to this three-bedroom home. The front entry is sheltered by a broad veranda. A bright country kitchen boasts an abundance of counter space and cupboards. Built-in amenities adorn the interior, including a pot shelf over the entry coat closet, an art niche, a skylight, and a walk-in pantry and island workstation in the kitchen. A box-bay window and a spa-style tub highlight the master suite. The two-car garage provides a workshop area.

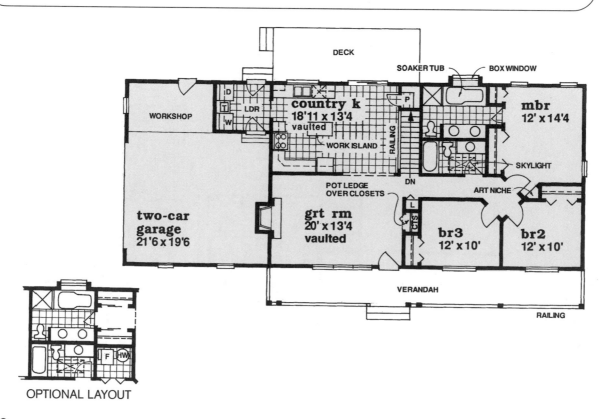

OPTIONAL LAYOUT

DESIGN
HPT890105

SQUARE FOOTAGE: 1,880
WIDTH: 88'-0" DEPTH: 42'-0"

THIS WIDE, WONDERFUL RANCH has it all: three bedrooms, full basement or crawl-space, formal dining room and a breakfast room in the country kitchen. All of this revolves around a central great room with a gas fireplace and media wall. The vaulted entry with plant ledges and a stunning window creates immediate impact. The master bedroom features a walk-in closet, soaking tub and separate shower. Both the master bedroom and Bedroom 2 present vaulted ceilings. The garage entry contains washer/dryer space and a walk-in pantry.

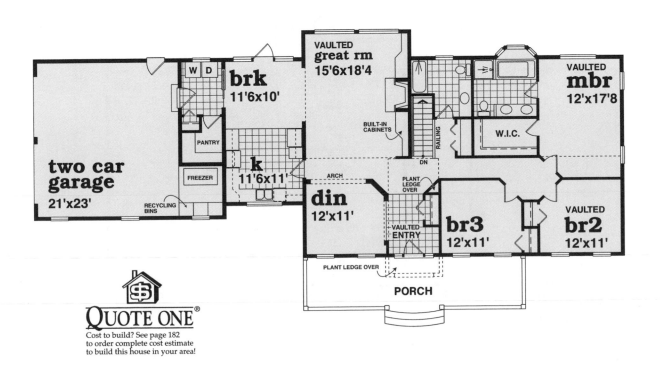

QUOTE ONE®
Cost to build? See page 182
to order complete cost estimate
to build this house in your area!

DESIGN
HPT890106

SQUARE FOOTAGE: 1,541
WIDTH: 87'-0" DEPTH: 44'-0"

THIS POPULAR DESIGN begins with a wraparound covered porch made even more charming with turned-wood spindles. The entry opens directly to the great room, which is warmed by a wood stove. The adjoining dining room offers access to a screened porch for outdoor after-dinner leisure. A country kitchen features a center island and a breakfast bay for casual meals. Family bedrooms share a full bath that features a soaking tub. The master suite offers a private bath and outdoor access. The two-car garage connects to the plan via the screened porch.

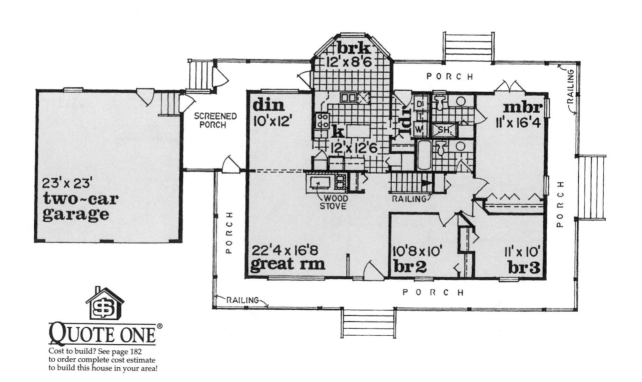

QUOTE ONE®
Cost to build? See page 182
to order complete cost estimate
to build this house in your area!

DESIGN
HPT890107

SQUARE FOOTAGE: 2,842
BONUS SPACE: 1,172 SQ. FT.
WIDTH: 91'-0" DEPTH: 69'-4"

THIS COUNTRY-STYLE home is lovely to behold and economical to build. Front and back covered porches create a warm transition to the yard, where a charming porte cochere gives shelter to those disembarking from vehicles. From the dining room, steps lead down to the sunken family room with a warming fireplace. A second set of steps leads up to the main hallway, which connects the living room with the master suite and two roomy bedrooms. The master bedroom features private access to the rear porch, two walk-in closets and a well-appointed bathroom. Room to grow is available in the unfinished space on the second floor.

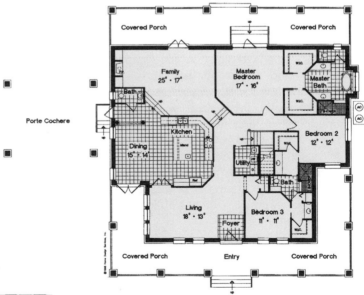

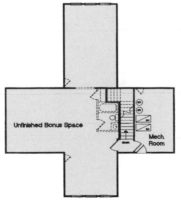

DESIGN
HPT890108

SQUARE FOOTAGE: 1,244
WIDTH: 44'-0" DEPTH: 62'-0"

COME HOME to the relaxed country style of this three-bedroom plan. A beautiful porch adorns the entire length of the front of the house—perfect for hanging plants. The entry opens directly to the hearth-warmed living room with built-in book-shelves and a wood box. The dining room sits open to the living room and the U-shaped kitchen, and features convenient access to the carport. To the right of the plan reside three bedrooms. Two family bedrooms share a full hall bath, while the master bedroom enjoys a private bath. Please specify crawlspace or slab founda-tion when ordering.

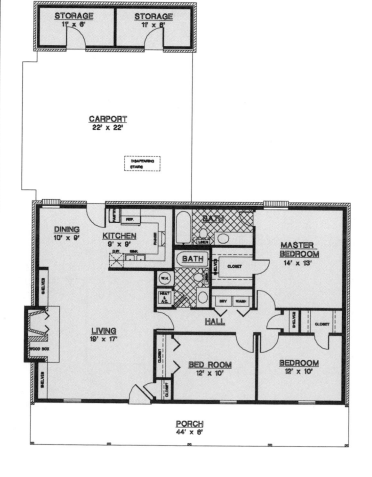

DESIGN
HPT890109

SQUARE FOOTAGE: 1,266
WIDTH: 40'-0" DEPTH: 64'-0"

THIS RUSTIC Craftsman-style cottage provides an open interior with good outdoor flow. The front covered porch invites casual gatherings, while inside, the dining area is set for both everyday and planned occasions. A centered fireplace in the great room shares its warmth with the dining room. A rear hall leads to the master suite and a secondary bedroom, while an upstairs loft has space for computers. Please specify crawlspace or slab foundation when ordering.

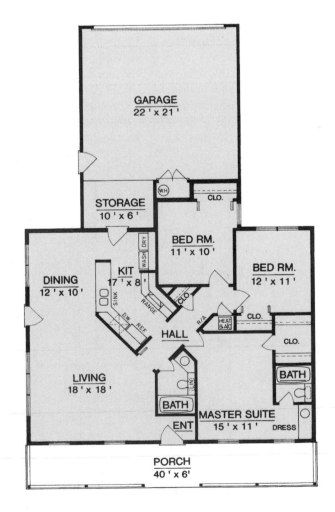

DESIGN
HPT890110

SQUARE FOOTAGE: 1,500
WIDTH: 64'-0" DEPTH: 45'-0"

THE EXPANSIVE covered front porch offers protection from the heat of the summer while providing a relaxing outdoor retreat. Graceful columns define the formal dining room and living room where a tray ceiling follows the contours created by the corner fireplace. The spacious kitchen is ready to serve the breakfast area, which enjoys views from its bay window. A utility room is conveniently located nearby along with access to the two-car garage. The left side of the home holds two family bedrooms sharing a full bath and a master bedroom with its own private bath—note all bedrooms include a walk-in closet.

Master Bedroom 14'6"x 13'

Porch

Breakfast 8'10"x 9'8"

Living 15'x 18'

Two Car Garage 18'x 20'

Bedroom 9'6"x 11'

Bedroom 9'6"x 11'

Dining 10'x 11'

Porch

DESIGN
HPT890111

SQUARE FOOTAGE: 2,270 SQ. FT.
BONUS SPACE: 461 SQ. FT.
WIDTH: 70'-0" DEPTH: 70'-0"

The charm and alluring nature of classic Victorian architecture comes to new life in this very up-to-date Texas design. Covered porches and a porte cochere drive-through add depth and dimension to the curb appeal of this home. Upon entry, the relationship between the living room area and the formal dining room brings a new twist in traditional layout, by introducing both spaces at an angle. The master suite enjoys living "on the water" with the pool up close. Generous His and Hers walk-in closets cap the well-appointed bath. No home built today would be complete without a home office or den, and this home sports one with French doors and a porch.

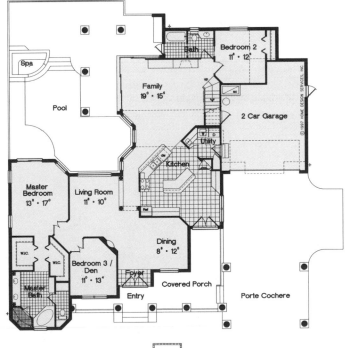

DESIGN
HPT890112

SQUARE FOOTAGE: 2,419
WIDTH: 85'-2" DEPTH: 46'-8"

LONG AND LOW, with brick siding and multi-pane shuttered windows, this ranch home is the picture of elegance. Enter through double doors to a sunken foyer and sunken living room with a fireplace. The dining room is beyond the living room and a step up. The family room, to the rear of the plan, features a fireplace and sliding glass doors to the rear patio. The kitchen provides a cooktop island and counter and cabinet space to suit any gourmet. The master bedroom enjoys a private terrace and bath with two vanities, a whirlpool tub and a separate shower. Two family bedrooms are to the front of the plan.

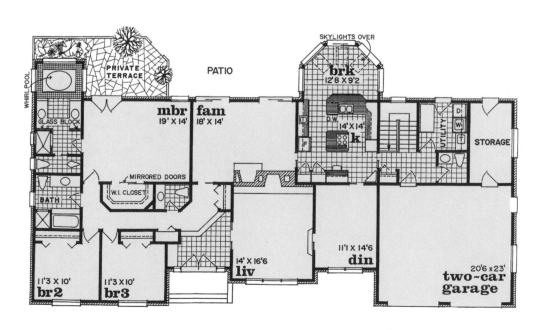

DESIGN
HPT890113

SQUARE FOOTAGE: 2,133
WIDTH: 74'-4" DEPTH: 58'-0"

THE DIAGONAL NATURE of this contemporary design makes it a versatile choice for a variety of lot arrangements. Inside, it is quite open visually. From the entry are exquisite views of the great room, with its fireplace flanked by windows, and of the stunning dining room. An island kitchen with a snack bar, planning desk and walk-in pantry adjoins the breakfast area. In the sleeping wing, a romantic master suite is accented with yard access, a whirlpool tub and a tiered ceiling. Two family bedrooms share a full hall bath. The three-car garage holds extra storage space and allows access to the house through the mud/laundry room.

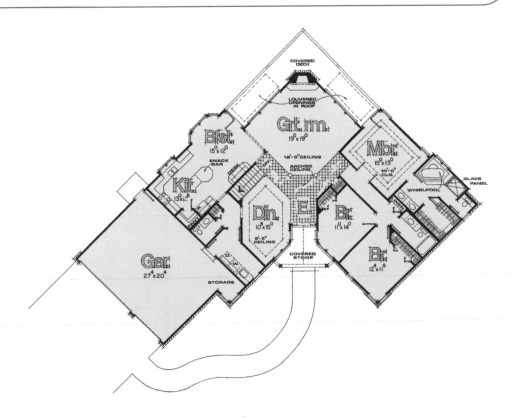

DESIGN
HPT890114

SQUARE FOOTAGE: 1,709
WIDTH: 70'-1" DEPTH: 60'-7"

This angled, country-style ranch is designed to adapt to just about any lot. Four bay windows and two dormers distinguish the exterior. A recessed, covered front porch opens to the foyer, which is visually connected to the adjoining great room. The "pavilion-style" great room, with windows at the front and rear, features a fireplace and built-ins. A dramatic angled kitchen with a snack bar faces the rear porch. A private master suite contains a tray ceiling, a dressing area, two closets and a compartmented five-fixture bath. A convenient half-bath is located off the foyer.

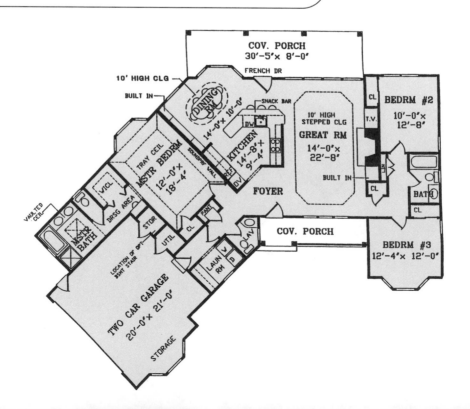

DESIGN
HPT890115

SQUARE FOOTAGE: 1,530
WIDTH: 73'-0" DEPTH: 30'-0"

THIS HOUSE BLENDS ancient and modern architectural styles into a harmony all its own. Skylights and solar panels on the roof bring the house right up to the present time. The drama of the portico is reflected by two interior columns, which frame the entrance to the cathedral living room. A heat-circulating firplace is to the right. The dining room and the kitchen area across the back of the house fills with an abundance of natural light. The bedroom wing features a large master suite with a private bath and two additional bedrooms that share a hall bath.

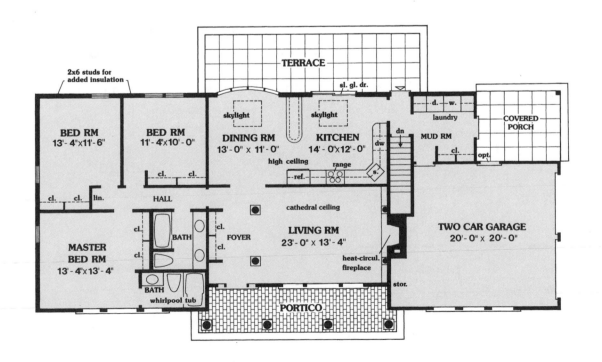

DESIGN
HPT890116

SQUARE FOOTAGE: 1,600
WIDTH: 75'-0" DEPTH: 37'-0"

TEXAS CHARM ABOUNDS in this one-story home with its covered porch, double dormers and combination of stone and siding. Inside, the entry opens to the living room with its beam-accented, vaulted ceiling and stone fireplace. The U-shaped kitchen adjoins the formal dining room where dividers offer privacy between the dining and living rooms. The master suite boasts a sitting room, walk-in closet and a private bath. On the left, two family bedrooms share a full bath. Please specify basement, crawlspace or slab foundation when ordering.

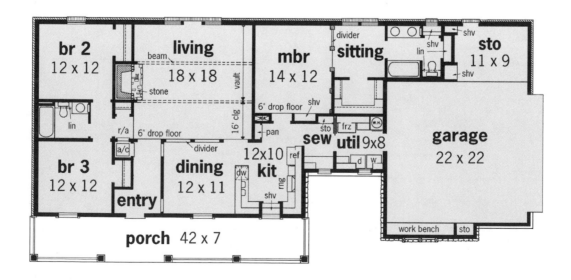

DESIGN
HPT890117

SQUARE FOOTAGE: 1,847
WIDTH: 49'-6" DEPTH: 72'-5"

A LONG COVERED PORCH invites relaxation after a hard day's work—sit back and enjoy the sunset. Inside, the foyer is flanked on either side by a family bedroom and a formal dining room. Straight ahead, the family room boasts a corner fireplace and access to the rear porch. The master bedroom is luxurious with a private bath, dressing room and walk-in closet. The two family bedrooms share a hall bath. The kitchen faces a bayed breakfast nook. A utility room and two-car garage with extra storage space complete this one-story design.

DESIGN
HPT890118

SQUARE FOOTAGE: 2,308
WIDTH: 67'-0" DEPTH: 56'-8"

HORIZONTAL SIDING combined with arch-top windows and a columned entry lend an exciting facade to this four-bedroom home. The foyer is entered through double doors and introduces the open dining and family-room area. The master suite occupies the left side of the plan and enjoys a sun-strewn sitting room, two walk-in closets and a luxurious bath complete with a garden tub and separate shower. The kitchen sits conveniently near the dining room and features a pantry, desk and view through the breakfast-nook windows. Two family bedrooms, sharing a full bath, reside near the kitchen. A third bedroom or guest suite is located by the family room. The family room contains a warming fireplace and media wall, which will make it a wonderful gathering place for the family.

DESIGN
HPT890119

SQUARE FOOTAGE: 1,590
WIDTH: 70'-4" DEPTH: 74'-0"

COLUMNS SEPARATE the foyer from the great room with its cathedral ceiling and fireplace. Serving meals has never been easier—the kitchen makes use of direct access to the dining room as well as a breakfast nook overlooking the deck and spa. A handy utility room even has room for a counter and cabinets. Three bedrooms make this an especially desirable design. The master bedroom, off of the great room, provides private access to the deck. This design is flexible enough to be accommodated by a narrow lot if the garage is relocated.

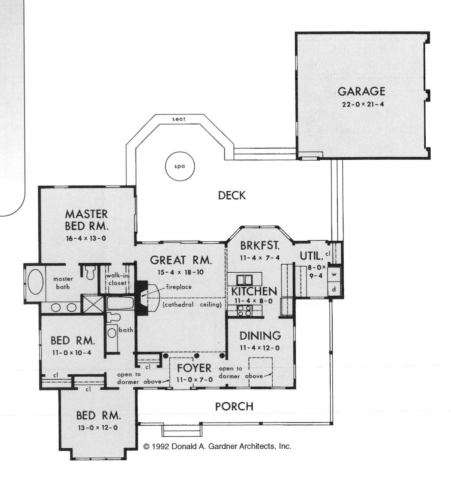

DESIGN
HPT890120

SQUARE FOOTAGE: 1,674
BONUS SPACE: 336 SQ. FT.
WIDTH: 56'-4" DEPTH: 50'-0"

A TRIO OF DORMERS, a metal porch covering and a mixture of stone and siding create a modern version of the traditional American home. The front porch is bordered by columns and features a trio of arches. A fireplace and built-ins, along with a cathedral ceiling that flows to the kitchen, highlight the great room. Tray ceilings crown the dining room and master bedroom, while visually expanding space. The bonus room makes a perfect playroom for kids, separating the noise from the common living areas and master bedroom. The master bath is complete with a sizable shower, double vanity, garden tub and a private privy.

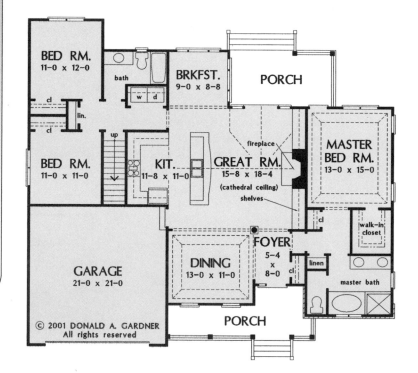

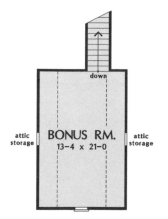

© 2001 Donald A. Gardner, Inc.

B. NATHAN

DESIGN
HPT890121

SQUARE FOOTAGE: 2,080
BONUS SPACE: 348 SQ. FT.
WIDTH: 63'-8"   DEPTH: 54'-4"

Architectural detail and traffic flow are the two most important elements in this design. A stone wall is enhanced by a box bay window that is capped with a metal roof. Stone visually anchors an additional box bay window. A prominent dormer features a Palladian-style window, which mimics the arches found on the front porch. Family efficiency is created by an open, yet defined floor plan. Decorative tray ceilings add custom appeal, while the flexibility of a study/bedroom provides options. Ample counter space is found in the utility/mud room and kitchen. Elegant doors lead into the master suite where dual walk-ins and vanities add to the suite experience.

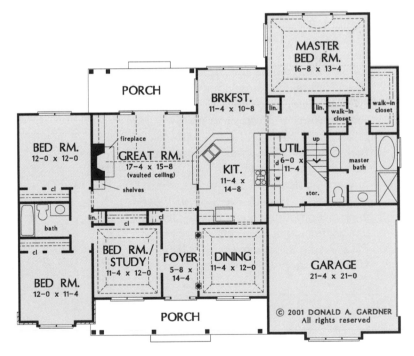

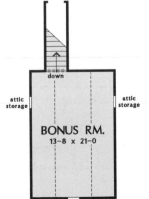

DESIGN
HPT890122

SQUARE FOOTAGE: 2,127
FUTURE SPACE: 1,095 SQ. FT.
WIDTH: 69'-0" DEPTH: 67'-4"

THIS HOME'S FACADE employs an elegant balance of country comfort and traditional grace. Inside, the foyer opens to the formal dining room that features a coffered ceiling. Straight ahead, the great room offers a warm fireplace and open flow to the breakfast and kitchen areas. Two secondary bedrooms and a full bath can be found just off the kitchen. A bonus room, near the master suite, can be used as a nursery or den. The private master bath enjoys dual vanities, two walk-in closets and a compartmented toilet. Upstairs, unfinished space is ready for expansion. Please specify basement, crawlspace or slab foundation when ordering.

Storage
4-11x12-6

Garage
21-7x21-5

Porch
9-0x21-6

Bath

Desk

Laun.
5-5x6-0

Owner's
Bedroom
14-3x15-11

Greatroom
18-7x15-11

Breakfast
12-7x10-1

Bedroom
13-3x11-0

Kitchen
12-7x11-3

Bath

Bath

Bonus Room
12-7x12-7

Foyer

Dining
12-7x11-2

Bedroom
13-3x10-2

Porch
32-8x6-0

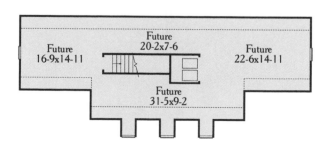

Future
16-9x14-11

Future
20-2x7-6

Future
22-6x14-11

Future
31-5x9-2

Donald A. Gardner Architects, Inc.

DESIGN
HPT890123

TOTAL: 3,040 SQ. FT.
LIVING BASEMENT: 1,736 SQ. FT.
WIDTH: 106'-5" DEPTH: 104'-2"

LOOKING A BIT LIKE A MOUNTAIN RESORT, this fine Craftsman home is sure to be the envy of your neighborhood. Entering through the elegant front door, one finds a spacious great room directly ahead. Here, a fireplace and a wall of windows give a cozy welcome. A lavish master suite begins with a sitting room complete with a fireplace and continues to a private porch, large walk-in closet and sumptuous bedroom area. The gourmet kitchen adjoins a sunny dining room and offers access to a screened porch.

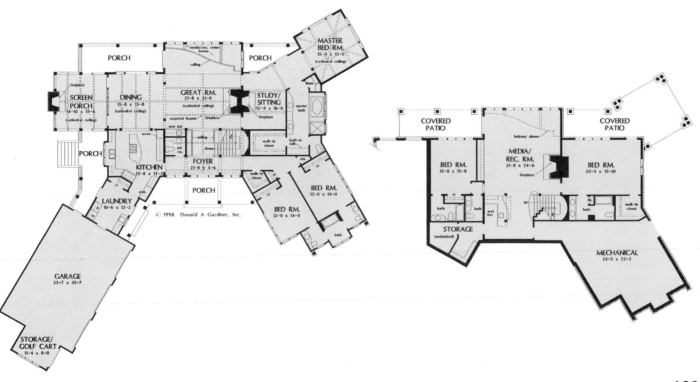

© 1998 Donald A Gardner, Inc.

DESIGN
HPT890124

SQUARE FOOTAGE: 3,188
BONUS SPACE: 615 SQ. FT.
WIDTH: 106'-4" DEPTH: 104'-1"

THIS INCREDIBLE HOME EVOKES IMAGES of stately Texas ranches with classic wood detailing and deep eaves. An arched entryway mimics the large clerestory above it, while a trio of dormers and multiple gables add architectural interest. Equally impressive, the interior boasts three fireplaces—one within a scenic screened porch—while a long cathedral ceiling extends from the great room to the screened porch and is highlighted by exposed beams. An art niche complements the foyer, and a wet bar enhances the great room. Columns help distinguish rooms without enclosing space. The extraordinary master suite features a large study/sitting area, bedroom with exposed beams in a hipped cathedral ceiling, huge walk-in closet and spacious master bath.

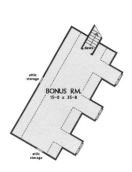

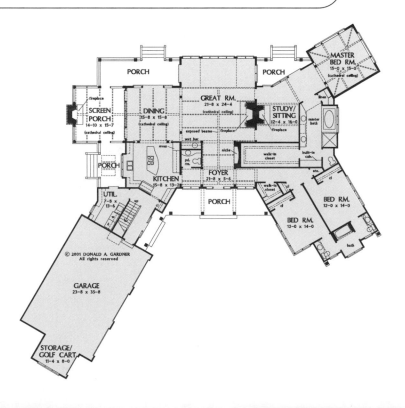

© 1999 Donald A. Gardner, Inc.

DESIGN
HPT890125

FIRST FLOOR: 3,555 SQ. FT.
SECOND FLOOR: 250 SQ. FT.
TOTAL: 3,805 SQ. FT.
BONUS SPACE: 490 SQ. FT.
WIDTH: 99'-8" DEPTH: 78'-8"

THIS EXTRAORDINARY FOUR-BEDROOM ESTATE features gables with decorative wood brackets, arched windows and a stone-and-siding facade for undeniable Craftsman character. At the heart of the home, a magnificent cathedral ceiling adds space and stature to the impressive great room, which accesses both back porches. Sharing the great room's cathedral ceiling, a loft makes an excellent reading nook. Tray ceilings adorn the dining room and library/media room, while all four bedrooms enjoy cathedral ceilings. A sizable kitchen is open to a large family room for ultimate togetherness. The master suite features back-porch access, a lavish private bath and an oversized walk-in closet. A spacious bonus room is located over the three-car garage for further expansion. There are three additional family bedrooms—one easily converts to a study.

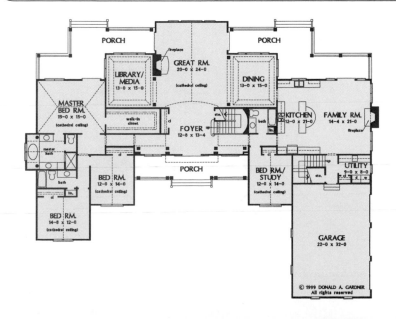

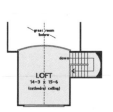

DESIGN
HPT890126

FIRST FLOOR: 2,477 SQ. FT.
SECOND FLOOR: 742 SQ. FT.
TOTAL: 3,219 SQ. FT.
BONUS SPACE: 419 SQ. FT.
WIDTH: 99'-10" DEPTH: 66'-2"

THIS ELEGANT DESIGN brings back the sophistication and elegance of days gone by, yet its modern layout creates a natural traffic flow to enhance easy living. Columns partition space without enclosing it, while built-ins in the great room and counter space in the utility/mud room add convenience. The family-efficient floor plan can be witnessed in the kitchen's handy pass-through, and the kitchen has porch access to the rear porch for outdoor entertaining. Cathedral ceilings highlight the master bedroom and bedroom/study, while vaulted ceilings top the breakfast area and loft/study. The bonus room can be used as a home theater, playroom or gym, and its position allows it to keep recreational noise away from the house proper.

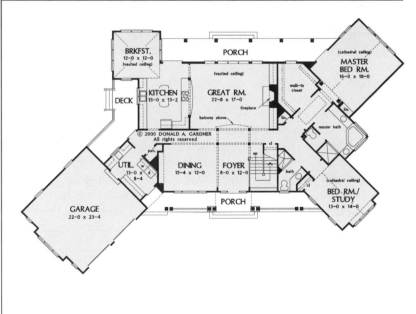

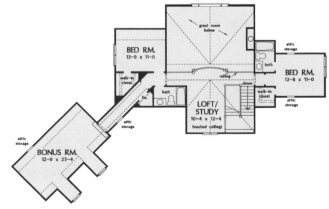

© 1999 Donald A. Gardner, Inc.

DESIGN
HPT890127

FIRST FLOOR: 1,662 SQ. FT.
SECOND FLOOR: 585 SQ. FT.
TOTAL: 2,247 SQ. FT.
FINISHED BASEMENT: 706 SQ. FT.
BONUS SPACE: 575 SQ. FT.
WIDTH: 81'-4" DEPTH: 68'-8"

A STUNNING center dormer with an arched window embellishes the exterior of this Craftsman-style home. The dormer's arched window allows light into the foyer and built-in niche. The second-floor hall is a balcony that overlooks both the foyer and great room. A generous back porch extends the great room, which features an impressive vaulted ceiling and fireplace, while a tray ceiling adorns the formal dining room. The master suite, which includes a tray ceiling as well, enjoys back-porch access, a built-in cabinet, generous walk-in closet and private bath. Two more bedrooms are located upstairs, while a fourth can be found in the basement along with a family room.

©1999 Donald A. Gardner, Inc.

DESIGN
HPT890128

97 Donald A Gardner Architects, Inc.

FIRST FLOOR: 1,743 SQ. FT.
SECOND FLOOR: 555 SQ. FT.
TOTAL: 2,298 SQ. FT.
BONUS SPACE: 350 SQ. FT.
WIDTH: 77'-11" DEPTH: 53'-2"

A LOVELY ARCH-TOP window and a wraparound porch set off this country exterior. Inside, the formal dining room opens off the foyer, which leads to a spacious great room. This living area has a fireplace and access to a screened porch with a cathedral ceiling. Bay windows allow natural light into the breakfast area and formal dining room. The master suite has a spacious bath and access to a private area of the rear porch. Two second-floor bedrooms share a bath and a balcony hall that offers an overlook to the great room.

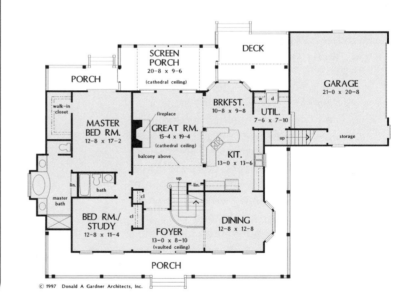

© 1997 Donald A Gardner Architects, Inc.

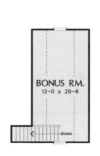

DESIGN
HPT890129

FIRST FLOOR: 1,499 SQ. FT.
SECOND FLOOR: 665 SQ. FT.
TOTAL: 2,164 SQ. FT.
BONUS SPACE: 380 SQ. FT.
WIDTH: 69'-8" DEPTH: 40'-6"

THE WARM DOWN-HOME appeal of this country house is as apparent inside as it is out. Inside, a two-story foyer and a great room with a hearth give the home an open feel. The great room leads to the breakfast area and the efficient kitchen with an island work area and a large pantry. The master bedroom is situated on the left side of the house for privacy. It features deck access, a large walk-in closet and a bath that includes dual vanities, a whirlpool tub and a separate shower. Three additional bedrooms, a full bath and bonus space are located upstairs.

QUOTE ONE®

Cost to build? See page 182
to order complete cost estimate
to build this house in your area!

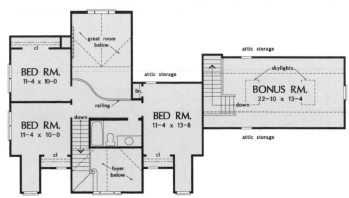

© 1992 Donald A. Gardner Architects, Inc.

DESIGN
HPT890130

FIRST FLOOR: 1,537 SQ. FT.
SECOND FLOOR: 641 SQ. FT.
TOTAL: 2,178 SQ. FT.
BONUS SPACE: 418 SQ. FT.
WIDTH: 65'-8" DEPTH: 70'-0"

THE WELCOMING CHARM of this farmhouse is expressed by its many windows and its covered wraparound porch. The two-story entrance foyer offers a Palladian window in a clerestory dormer that casts warm natural light on a wood-trimmed interior. The first-floor master suite, thoughtfully positioned for privacy and accessibility, features a U-shaped walk-in closet and a private bath with a bumped-out tub and twin vanities. The second floor has two bedrooms, a full bath and plenty of storage.

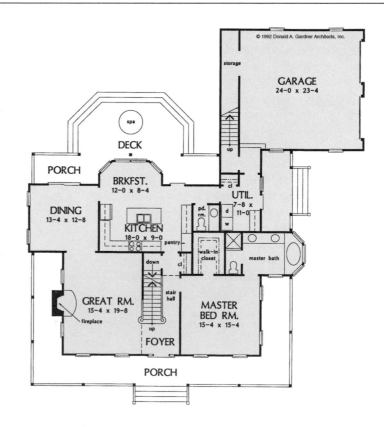

© 1992 Donald A. Gardner Architects, Inc.

GARAGE
24-0 x 23-4

storage

PORCH

DECK

spa

BRKFST.
12-0 x 8-4

DINING
13-4 x 12-8

KITCHEN
18-0 x 9-0

pantry

UTIL.
7-8 x 11-0

pd. rm.

walk-in closet

master bath

GREAT RM.
15-4 x 19-8

fireplace

down

stair hall

MASTER BED RM.
15-4 x 15-4

up

FOYER

PORCH

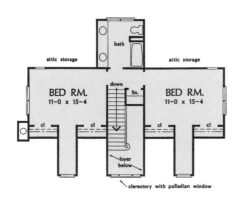

attic storage

bath

attic storage

BED RM.
11-0 x 15-4

down

lin.

BED RM.
11-0 x 15-4

cl

cl

cl

cl

foyer below

clerestory with palladian window

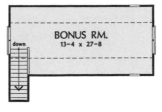

BONUS RM.
13-4 x 27-8

down

Quote One®

Cost to build? See page 182
to order complete cost estimate
to build this house in your area!

DESIGN
HPT890131

FIRST FLOOR: 1,724 SQ. FT.
SECOND FLOOR: 728 SQ. FT.
TOTAL: 2,452 SQ. FT.
WIDTH: 61'-4" DEPTH: 46'-6"

OUTDOOR LIVING takes a beautiful turn in this lovely home. The interior is just as great—bay windows in the breakfast room and master bath, dormers and arched rear windows, and an incredible sun room with a hot tub and glass roof. The spacious great room features a fireplace, cathedral ceiling and clerestory with arched window. The master bath complements the master bedroom with a garden tub, separate shower, double-bowl vanity and walk-in closet. Two bedrooms share the upper level with a study/loft overlooking the great room. This study area could be converted into a fourth bedroom.

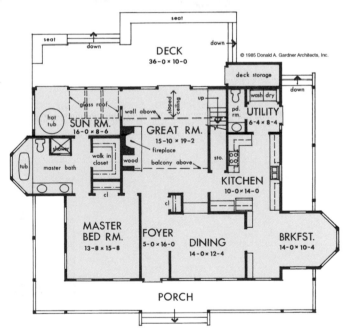

© 1985 Donald A. Gardner Architects, Inc.

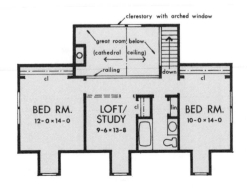

DESIGN
HPT890132

FIRST FLOOR: 1,501 SQ. FT.
SECOND FLOOR: 631 SQ. FT.
TOTAL: 2,132 SQ. FT.
WIDTH: 76'-0" DEPTH: 48'-4"

THIS HOME REVEALS its rustic charm with a metal roof, dormers and exposed column rafters. The full-length porch is an invitation to comfortable living inside. The great room shares a fireplace with the spacious dining room that has rear-porch access. The kitchen is this home's focus, with plenty of counter and cabinet space, a window sink and an open layout. The first-floor master suite features two walk-in closets and a grand bath. Two family bedrooms and a playroom reside on the second floor. Please specify basement, crawlspace or slab foundation when ordering.

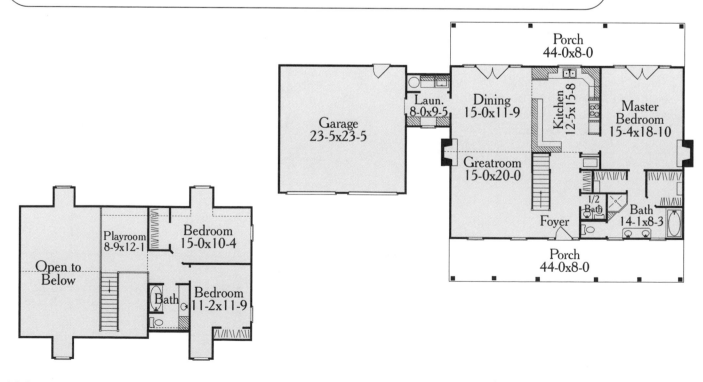

DESIGN
HPT890133

FIRST FLOOR: 1,855 SQ. FT.
SECOND FLOOR: 1,241 SQ. FT.
TOTAL: 3,096 SQ. FT.
WIDTH: 82'-0" DEPTH: 50'-0" **L D**

WITH ITS CLASSIC farmhouse good looks and just-right floor plan, this country residence has it all. The wraparound covered porch at the entry gives way to a long foyer with an open staircase. The living room with a fireplace and the formal dining room open to the left. The extensive country kitchen pampers the chef with a cooktop island and hearth. A spectacular private bath with a separate dressing room, whirlpool tub and huge walk-in closet completes the master suite. The second floor has a total of two bedrooms, one with a walk-in closet and a full bath. A bedroom/sitting room with a built-in desk divides the two bedrooms. A full hall bath is located at the top of the staircase to the far right.

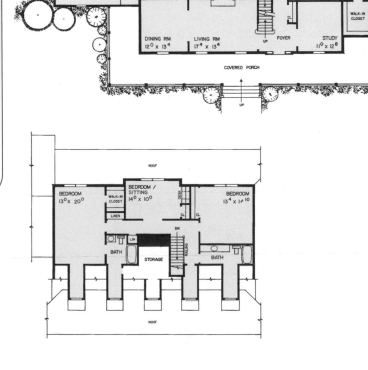

QUOTE ONE®
Cost to build? See page 182
to order complete cost estimate
to build this house in your area!

DESIGN
HPT890134

FIRST FLOOR: 2,092 SQ. FT.
SECOND FLOOR: 1,027 SQ. FT.
TOTAL: 3,119 SQ. FT.
WIDTH: 66'-0" DEPTH: 80'-0"

THIS WELL-THOUGHT-OUT PLAN allows for household members to plan separate events in one evening. The family room and the living room/library both feature a fireplaces and built-ins. The pass-through kitchen includes an island and connects the breakfast area and dining room. Accessible to the covered porch, the master bedroom provides a full private bath and His and Her closets. The second floor has three additional bedrooms and a balcony overlooking the first-floor family room. The two-car garage completes the plan.

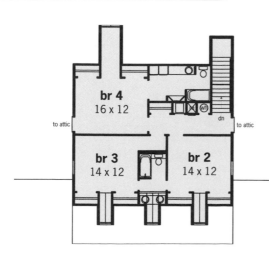

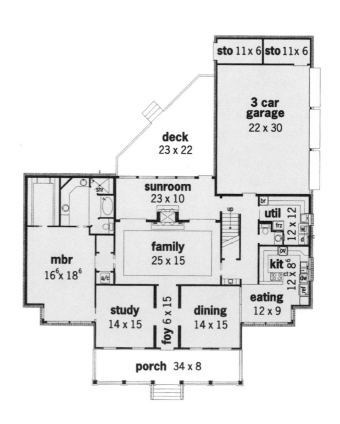

DESIGN
HPT890135

FIRST FLOOR: 3,079 SQ. FT.
SECOND FLOOR: 813 SQ. FT.
TOTAL: 3,892 SQ. FT.
WIDTH: 75'-4" DEPTH: 80'-8"

THE USE OF COLUMNS and dormers on this home's facade conjures up images of elegant days past. As you enter the foyer of this beautiful home, large dining and living rooms welcome you on either side. A magnificent family room with a fireplace is perfect for spending quality time with your family on cold nights. French doors allow access to a covered patio at the rear of the plan. A powder room for your guests is located just off the foyer to the right. Across from the dining room is the entrance to the gourmet kitchen and breakfast nook. The kitchen features an island counter and a pantry. The master suite boasts French doors to the backyard, a private bath with a whirlpool tub, shower, dual vanities and spacious His and Hers walk-in closets. Please specify basement or slab foundation when ordering.

DESIGN
HPT890136

FIRST FLOOR: 2,142 SQ. FT.
SECOND FLOOR: 960 SQ. FT.
TOTAL: 3,102 SQ. FT.
BONUS SPACE: 327 SQ. FT.
WIDTH: 75'-8" DEPTH: 53'-0"

A HIPPED ROOF—with three petite dormers—accents the long covered porch of this fine four-bedroom home. Inside, the foyer is flanked by the formal living and dining rooms. The spacious family room features a warming fireplace and built-in bookcases. The kitchen offers plenty of cabinet and counter space, as well as a large island with a sink, a walk-in pantry, a built-in desk and a butler's pantry. The adjacent breakfast area is filled with natural light from three walls of windows. The first-floor master suite provides a huge walk-in closet and a pampering bath. Upstairs, three bedrooms share two full baths, and future expansion needs can be met by the recreation room on this level.

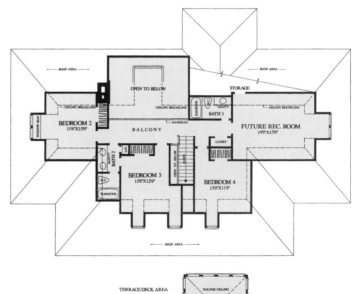

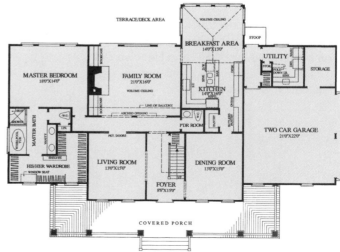

DESIGN
HPT890137

SQUARE FOOTAGE: 2,777
BONUS SPACE: 818 SQ. FT.
WIDTH: 75'-6"   DEPTH: 60'-2"

COLUMNS LINE a covered front porch, which is topped by three dormers, and brick combines with siding to give this home a warm and welcoming feeling. Inside, the foyer introduces the formal dining room to the left, defined by yet more columns. Directly ahead lies the living room, enhanced by a fireplace and built-in shelves. The efficient kitchen features a walk-in pantry, a built-in desk and a wonderful island—complete with a sink. The nearby family room and breakfast area are suffused with light from a multitude of windows. Two family bedrooms share a full bath, while the master suite pampers with privacy. The upstairs is available for future expansion.

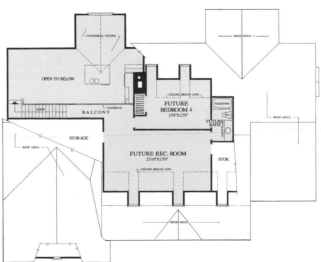

DESIGN
HPT890138

FIRST FLOOR: 1,320 SQ. FT.
SECOND FLOOR: 552 SQ. FT.
TOTAL: 1,872 SQ. FT.
WIDTH: 56'-0" DEPTH: 61'-0"

THIS UNIQUE ROOFING style captures your attention and the varying rooflines hold your interest. The foyer is open to the dining room on the left and the living room on the right. A large family room is straight ahead, featuring a built-in bookshelf and fireplace. The efficient kitchen offers plenty of counter space in a relatively small area. A wall of windows in the eating room allows light to billow into this home. The master suite includes a bath and walk-in closets. Large front and rear porches provide extensive opportunity for outdoor entertaining. Please specify basement, crawlspace or slab foundation when ordering.

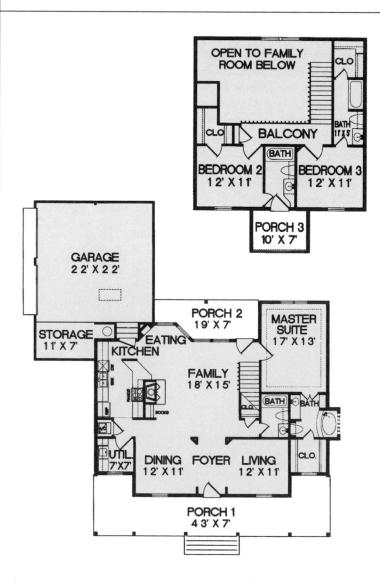

DESIGN
HPT890139

FIRST FLOOR: 1,667 SQ. FT.
SECOND FLOOR: 803 SQ. FT.
TOTAL: 2,470 SQ. FT.
BONUS SPACE: 318 SQ. FT.
WIDTH: 52'-4" DEPTH: 57'-0"

COUNTRY ACCENTS and farmhouse style enhance the facade of this lovely two-story home. The first floor provides a formal dining room and great room warmed by a fireplace. The kitchen connects to a breakfast bay—perfect for casual morning meals. The first-floor master suite includes two walk-in closets and a private bath. Upstairs, a loft overlooks the two-story great room. Three second-floor bedrooms share a hall bath. The bonus room above the garage is great for a home office or guest suite.

DESIGN
HPT890140

FIRST FLOOR: 1,374 SQ. FT.
SECOND FLOOR: 600 SQ. FT.
TOTAL: 1,974 SQ. FT.
WIDTH: 51'-8" DEPTH: 50'-8" **L D**

BALUSTRADES and brackets, dual balconies and a wraparound porch create a country-style exterior reminiscent of soft summer evenings spent watching fireflies and sipping sun tea. The tiled foyer opens to the two-story great room filled with light from six windows and a fireplace. The sunny bayed nook shares its natural light with the snack counter and kitchen. A spacious master suite occupies a bay window and offers a sumptuous bath. Upstairs, two family bedrooms—each with a private balcony and a walk-in closet—share a full bath.

DESIGN
HPT890141

SQUARE FOOTAGE: 2,092
WIDTH: 85'-9" DEPTH: 67'-10" L

STUCCO EXTERIOR WALLS highlighted by simple window treatment and effective glass-block patterns introduce a fine, western-style home. High ceilings and open planning contribute to the spaciousness of the interior. The large foyer effectively routes traffic to the main living areas. To the left is the angular formal dining room with its half walls and tray ceiling. Straight ahead from the double front doors is the formal living room. It has a high viga, or beamed ceiling, and a commanding corner fireplace with a raised hearth and banco, or bench. French doors open to the covered rear patio. Past the built-in bookshelves of the family room is the hallway to the sleeping zone.

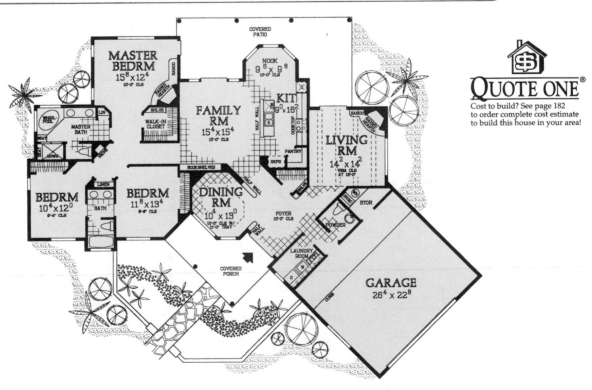

QUOTE ONE®
Cost to build? See page 182
to order complete cost estimate
to build this house in your area!

DESIGN
HPT890142

SQUARE FOOTAGE: 2,000
WIDTH: 75'-0" DEPTH: 55'-0"

THIS CLASSIC STUCCO design provides a cool retreat in any climate. From the covered porch, enter the skylit foyer to find an arched ceiling leading to the central gathering room with its raised-hearth fireplace and terrace access. A connecting corner dining room is conveniently located near the amenity-filled kitchen. The large master suite includes terrace access and a private bath with a whirlpool tub, a separate shower and plenty of closet space. A second bedroom and a study that can be converted to a bedroom complete this wonderful plan.

Quote One®

Cost to build? See page 182 to order complete cost estimate to build this house in your area!

DESIGN
HPT890143

SQUARE FOOTAGE: 2,624
WIDTH: 88'-8" DEPTH: 69'-0" L

ANGLED LIVING SPACES add interest to this already magnificent Santa Fe home. From the offset entry you can travel straight back to the open gathering room—or turn to the right to enter the formal living and dining rooms. The huge kitchen is centralized and features an L-shaped work area with an island. Secondary bedrooms open to a side patio and share a full bath. The master suite is complemented by a warm study and is separated from the secondary bedrooms for privacy.

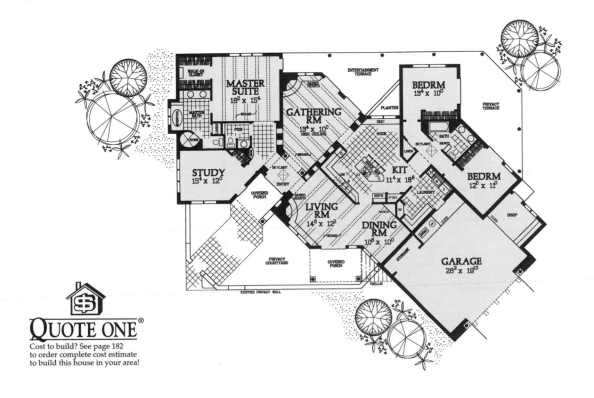

QUOTE ONE®
Cost to build? See page 182
to order complete cost estimate
to build this house in your area!

DESIGN
HPT890144

SQUARE FOOTAGE: 2,741
WIDTH: 98'-0" DEPTH: 59'-0"

THE TWO-LEVEL REAR PATIO brings a new dimension to outdoor living. Patio access is from the foyer, family room and great room. The family room features a corner fireplace with a raised hearth, and a snack bar off the U-shaped kitchen, which has an island cooktop and a walk-in pantry. A second fireplace, also with a raised hearth, warms the great room. The master suite opens to a private courtyard and includes a compartmented bath with separate shower and garden tub, a double-bowl vanity and a walk-in closet. Two family bedrooms at the front of the plan offer walk-in closets and share a bath.

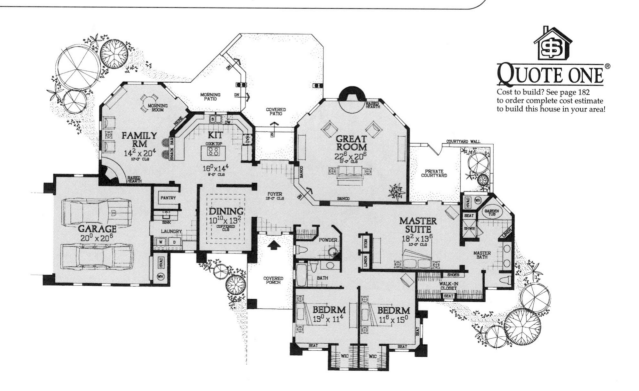

QUOTE ONE®
Cost to build? See page 182
to order complete cost estimate
to build this house in your area!

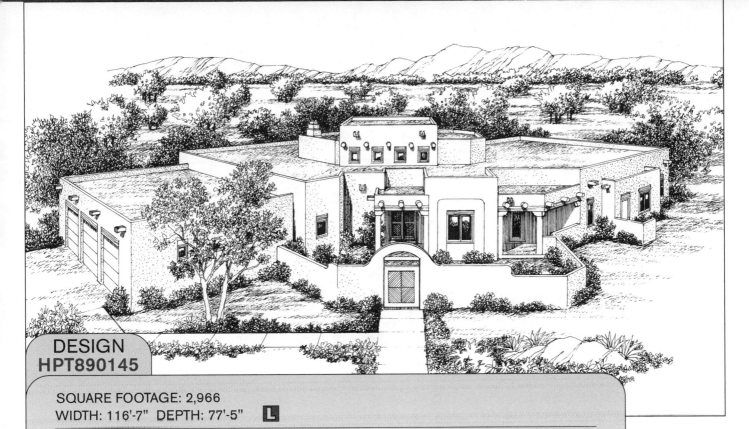

DESIGN
HPT890145

SQUARE FOOTAGE: 2,966
WIDTH: 116'-7" DEPTH: 77'-5" L

HERE'S A RAMBLING RANCH with a unique configuration. Massive double doors at the front entrance are sheltered by the covered porch. This well-zoned plan offers exceptional one-story livability for the active family. The central foyer routes traffic effectively while featuring a feeling of spaciousness. Note the dramatic columns that accentuate the big living room with its high 17'-8" ceiling. This interesting, angular room has a commanding corner fireplace with a raised hearth, a wall of windows, a doorway to the huge rear covered porch and a pass-through to the kitchen. The informal family room directly accesses the rear porch and is handy to the three children's bedrooms. At the opposite end of the plan, and guaranteed its full measure of privacy, is the large master suite. The master bedroom, with its high ceiling, enjoys direct access to the rear porch.

QUOTE ONE®
Cost to build? See page 182
to order complete cost estimate
to build this house in your area!

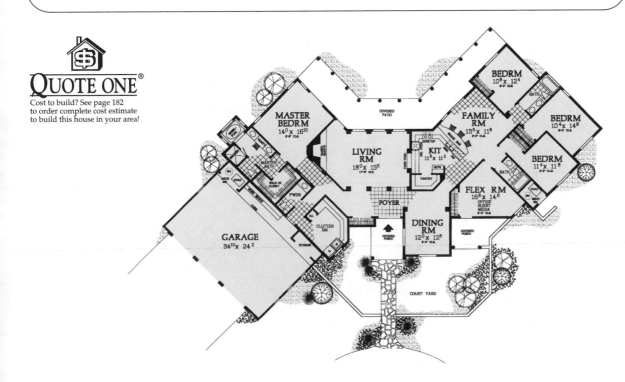

DESIGN
HPT890146

SQUARE FOOTAGE: 2,582
WIDTH: 87'-4" DEPTH: 65'-10"

THIS HOME IS MADE TO ORDER for a slightly sloping lot—or have your site graded to fit its contours! The classic Pueblo styling includes projecting vigas, rounded corners and rough-sawn lintels. Enter by way of a walled courtyard that protects the entry. The central foyer gives way to a large living room (there's space for a baby grand!) and the bedrooms on the right. The master suite opens to a private covered patio and has a bath with a gigantic walk-in closet, a garden tub and a separate shower. The formal dining room features a covered patio for alfresco meals and connects to the island kitchen for easy entertaining. For casual occasions, the family room serves up a corner fireplace and access to yet another patio area. The two-car garage includes plenty of storage space.

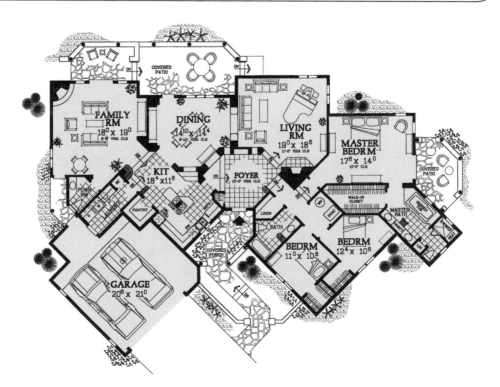

Cost to build? See page 182
to order complete cost estimate
to build this house in your area!

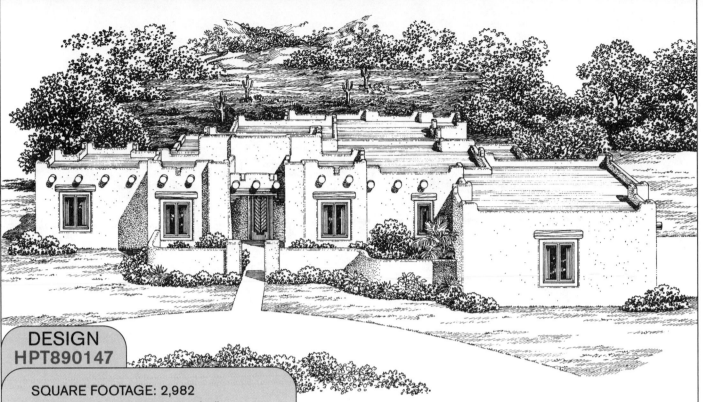

DESIGN
HPT890147

SQUARE FOOTAGE: 2,982
WIDTH: 88'-6" **DEPTH:** 104'-0"

THIS SOUTHWESTERN design represents the best of past and present. The exterior recalls the early architecture of the region when it was newly settled, while the interior caters to present-day tastes. The focal point of the sunken living room is the corner fireplace. The gourmet kitchen boasts a cooktop island, skylight, breakfast nook and access to a covered porch. On the opposite side of the plan, two family bedrooms share a bath and a study, with access to a covered porch. The master suite, at the rear of the home, boasts a corner fireplace, two walk-in closets, a luxurious bath, and a door to a private section of the covered porch.

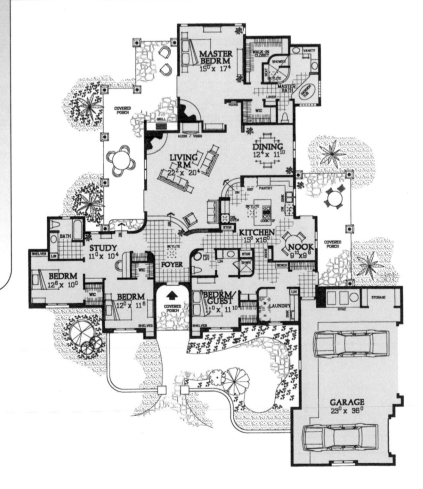

DESIGN
HPT890148

SQUARE FOOTAGE: 3,169
WIDTH: 120'-0" DEPTH: 76'-0" 🇱

PROJECTING WOOD BEAMS—called vigas—add a distinctive touch to this Santa Fe exterior. A private courtyard leads to the entryway of this radially planned home. To the left of the foyer rests a living room with a wood-beamed ceiling, music alcove and fireplace. Past the formal dining room on the right is the family room and large country kitchen with snack bar and morning room. The focal point of this casual living zone is the massive fireplace with three separate fire boxes—the center of the plan's radius. Three family bedrooms, two full baths and an open study with adjoining courtyard round out the right wing. Wood beams and an oversized, spa-style bath give the master suite a posh attitude. Completing this wing is an office, powder room, laundry/utility room and a three-car garage with work room.

🏠
QUOTE ONE®
Cost to build? See page 182
to order complete cost estimate
to build this house in your area!

DESIGN
HPT890149

SQUARE FOOTAGE: 3,428
WIDTH: 120'-0" DEPTH: 86'-0"

AN IN-LINE FLOOR PLAN follows the tradition of the original Santa Fe-style homes. The slight curve to the overall configuration lends an interesting touch. From the front courtyard, the plan opens to a formal living room and dining room, complemented by a family room and a kitchen with an adjoining morning room. The master suite is found to one side of the plan while family bedrooms share space at the opposite end. There's also a huge office and a bonus/study area for private times.

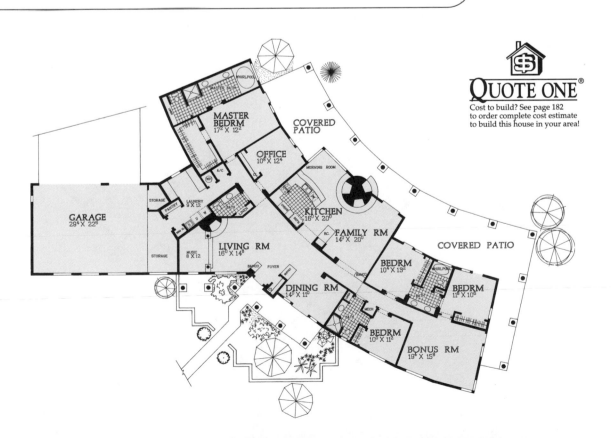

QUOTE ONE®
Cost to build? See page 182
to order complete cost estimate
to build this house in your area!

DESIGN
HPT890150

SQUARE FOOTAGE: 2,226
WIDTH: 103'-1" DEPTH: 71'-11" **L**

THE IMPRESSIVE, DOUBLE-DOOR ENTRY to the walled courtyard sets the tone for this Santa Fe masterpiece home. The expansive great room shows off its casual style with a centerpiece fireplace and abundant windows overlooking the patio. Joining the great room is the formal dining room, again graced with windows and patio doors. The large gourmet kitchen has an eat-in snack bar and joins the family room to create a warm atmosphere for casual entertaining. Family-room extras include a fireplace, entertainment built-ins and double doors to the front courtyard. Just off the family room are the two large family bedrooms, which share a private bath. The relaxing master suite is located off the great room and has double doors to the back patio.

QUOTE ONE®

Cost to build? See page 182
to order complete cost estimate
to build this house in your area!

DESIGN
HPT890151

SQUARE FOOTAGE: 2,922
WIDTH: 82'-0" DEPTH: 77'-0"

THIS ONE-STORY HOME matches traditional Southwestern design elements such as stucco, tile and exposed rafters (called vigas) with an up-to-date floor plan. The forty-three-foot gathering room provides a dramatic multi-purpose living area. Interesting angles highlight the kitchen, which offers plenty of counter and cabinet space, a planning desk, a snack-bar pass-through into the gathering room, and a morning room with a bumped-out bay. A media room could serve as a third bedroom. The luxurious master bedroom contains a walk-in closet and an amenity-filled bath with a whirlpool tub. A three-car garage easily serves the family fleet.

QUOTE ONE®
Cost to build? See page 182
to order complete cost estimate
to build this house in your area!

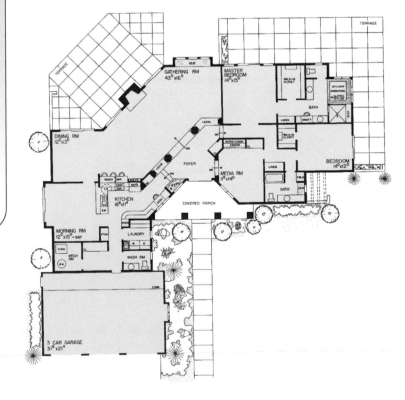

DESIGN
HPT890152

SQUARE FOOTAGE: 3,212
WIDTH: 108'-0" DEPTH: 57'-0"   L

THIS ONE-STORY HOME pairs the customary tile and stucco of Spanish design with a very livable floor plan. The sunken living room with its open-hearth fireplace promises to be a cozy gathering place. For more casual occasions, there's a welcoming family room with a fireplace off the foyer. The kitchen works well with the formal dining room and nearby breakfast room, which offers access to the rear terrace. Two secondary bedrooms share a large full hall bath while a sumptuous master suite enjoys a huge walk-in closet, a whirlpool tub, a separate shower and a romantic fireplace.

QUOTE ONE®
Cost to build? See page 182
to order complete cost estimate
to build this house in your area!

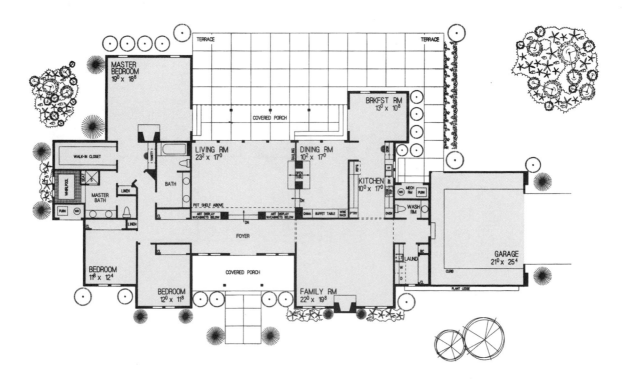

DESIGN
HPT890153

SQUARE FOOTAGE: 2,850
WIDTH: 86'-0" DEPTH: 69'-0" [L]

THIS SOUTHWESTERN design caters to families who enjoy outdoor living and entertaining. Doors open onto a shaded terrace from the master bedroom and living room, while a sliding glass door in the family room accesses a smaller terrace. Outdoor entertaining is a breeze with the outdoor bar with pass-through window to the kitchen. In the sleeping wing, two secondary bedrooms share a hall bath with a dual-bowl vanity, while the master suite is designed to pamper the fortunate homeowner with such amenities as a corner fireplace, His and Hers walk-in closets, a whirlpool tub, a separate shower and a separate vanity.

QUOTE ONE®
Cost to build? See page 182 to order complete cost estimate to build this house in your area!

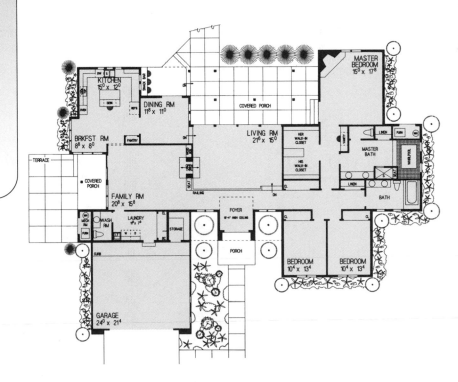

DESIGN
HPT890154

SQUARE FOOTAGE: 2,966
WIDTH: 114'-10" DEPTH: 79'-2" [L]

THE DRAMATIC ENTRANCE of this grand Sun Country home gives way to interesting angles and optimum livability inside. Columns frame the formal living room which provides views of the rear grounds from the foyer. The private master bedroom is contained on the left portion of the plan. Here, a relaxing master bath provides an abundance of amenities that include a walk-in closet, a bumped-out whirlpool tub, a separate shower and a double-bowl vanity. A clutter room and powder room complete this wing. Centrally located for efficiency, the kitchen easily serves the living room—via a pass-through—as well as the formal dining room, family room and flex room. Three secondary bedrooms share two full baths.

QUOTE ONE®

Cost to build? See page 182
to order complete cost estimate
to build this house in your area!

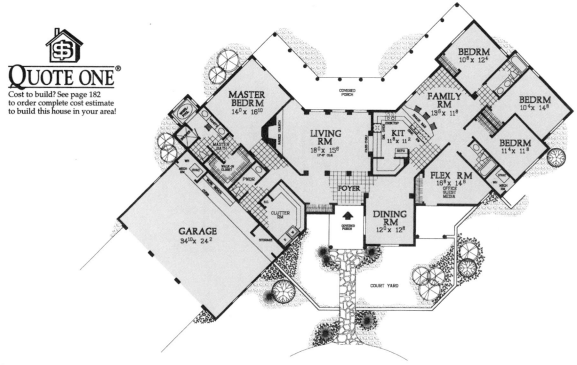

DESIGN
HPT890155

SQUARE FOOTAGE: 3,056
WIDTH: 112'-8" DEPTH: 80'-0" **L**

THIS ONE-STORY HOME is spiced with authentic Spanish flavor. Striking a note of distinction, the arched privacy walls provide a fine backdrop for the long, raised planter. The low-pitched roof features tile and has a wide overhang with exposed rafter tails. The interior is thoughtfully planned. The welcoming family room is flanked by the sleeping wing and the living wing. Indoor-outdoor relationships are outstanding, further enhancing the plan. The spacious interior court adds a sense of peace to the design. The sleeping facilities include three family bedrooms and a master suite located to the rear for privacy.

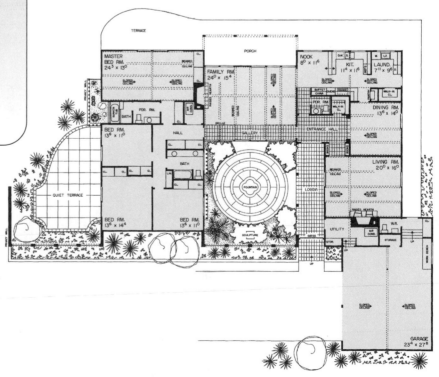

DESIGN
HPT890156

SQUARE FOOTAGE: 2,086
WIDTH: 82'-0" DEPTH: 58'-4"

A MAJESTIC FACADE makes this home pleasing to view. This home provides dual-use space in the wonderful sunken sitting room and media area. The kitchen has a breakfast bay and overlooks the snack bar to the sunken family area. A few steps from the kitchen is the formal dining room, which functions well with the upper patio. Two family bedrooms share a full bath. The private master suite includes a sitting area and French doors that open to a private covered patio.

QUOTE ONE®
Cost to build? See page 182
to order complete cost estimate
to build this house in your area!

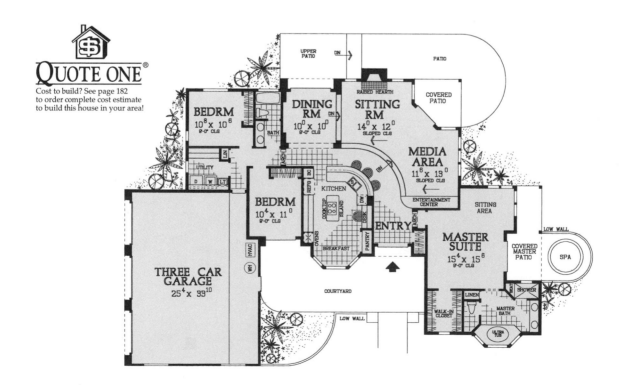

J.N. HANSEN

DESIGN
HPT890157

SQUARE FOOTAGE: 2,397
WIDTH: 60'-0" DEPTH: 71'-8"

LOW-SLUNG HIPPED rooflines and an abundance of glass enhance the unique exterior of this sunny one-story home. Inside, the use of soffits and tray ceilings heighten the distinctive style of the floor plan. To the left, double doors lead to the private master bedroom, which is bathed in natural light. Convenient planning of the gourmet kitchen places everything at minimal distances and allows serving the outdoor summer kitchen, breakfast nook and family room with equal ease.

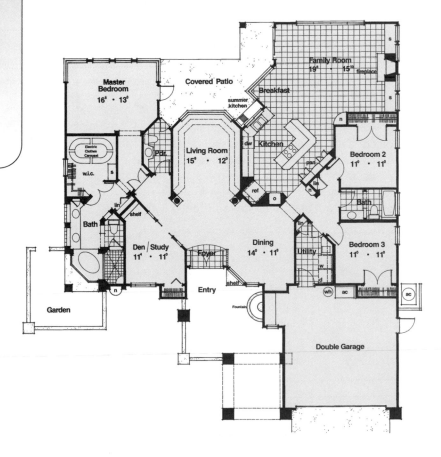

DESIGN
HPT890158

SQUARE FOOTAGE: 2,397
WIDTH: 73'-2" DEPTH: 73'-2"

DRAMATIC ROOFLINES and a unique entrance set the mood of this contemporary home. Double doors lead into the foyer, which opens directly to the formal living and dining rooms. A den/study is adjacent to this area and offers a quiet retreat. The spacious kitchen features a large cooktop work island and plenty of counter and cabinet space. The spacious family room expands this area and features a wall of windows and a warming fireplace. Two secondary bedrooms share a full bath. The master suite is designed with pleasure in mind. Included in the suite are a lavish bath and a deluxe walk-in closet, as well as access to the covered patio.

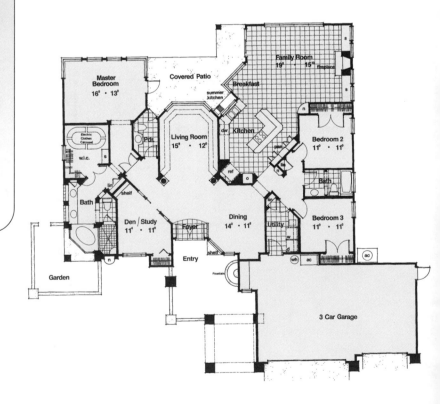

DESIGN
HPT890159

SQUARE FOOTAGE: 2,005
WIDTH: 58'-0" DEPTH: 60'-0"

VAULTED AND VOLUME ceilings soar above well-designed living areas in this spectacular move-up home. Open spaces create interior vistas and invite both formal and informal gatherings. An elegant dining room, defined by columns, offers views to the front property through multi-level muntin windows. To the left of the foyer, an extensive living room offers plans for an optional fireplace as well as privacy for quiet gatherings. The great room offers a vaulted ceiling and views to outdoor areas, and opens to the breakfast room with patio access and the kitchen with its angled counter. Two family bedrooms, each with a volume ceiling, and a bath with twin lavatories complete the right side of the plan. The master bedroom enjoys its own bath with a whirlpool tub, separate shower, dual vanity and compartmented toilet.

DESIGN
HPT890160

SQUARE FOOTAGE: 1,433
WIDTH: 40'-0" DEPTH: 55'-0"

A VOLUME ENTRY and open planning give this house a feeling of spaciousness that goes far beyond its modest square footage. The foyer opens onto a large living and dining area that combines for flexible entertaining needs. The kitchen is planned to fulfill a gourmet's dream and merges with the breakfast area for informal dining. Located to the rear for privacy, the master suite opens onto the patio and features a lush bath with a huge walk-in closet. Two secondary bedrooms share a full hall bath. The covered rear patio has a dramatic vaulted ceiling, giving an extra touch of elegance to casual living.

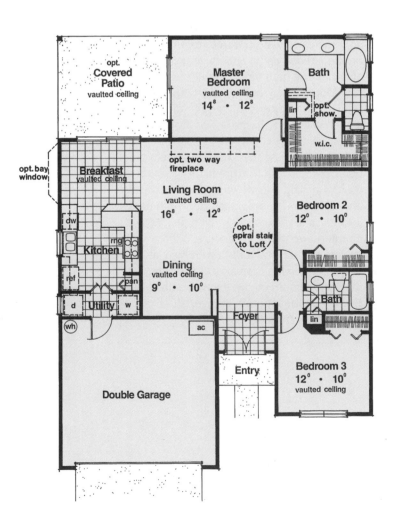

DESIGN
HPT890161

SQUARE FOOTAGE: 2,010
WIDTH: 62'-8" DEPTH: 56'-0"

THE CONTEMPORARY use of glass defines this dramatic exterior, but the real excitement begins with the interior design. A private living room offers a quiet place for formal entertaining and important conversations. The dining room, just across the foyer, offers views and light from graceful, arch-topped muntin windows and opens to a gallery hall, with the kitchen just steps away. For informal gatherings, the family room offers a warming fireplace, built-in shelves for an entertainment center or library, and views and access to a covered patio. The secluded master suite offers a generous bath with a garden tub. Three family bedrooms share a full bath and access to the covered patio. Plans for this home include a choice of two exterior elevations.

DESIGN
HPT890162

SQUARE FOOTAGE: 1,624
WIDTH: 52'-0"   DEPTH: 50'-6"

THIS AFFORDABLE RANCH home offers fine stucco detailing. The entry features transom windows, which bathe the plant ledge in natural light. The living room has a vaulted ceiling, a fireplace and rear-yard access. The formal dining room provides tall, arched windows and easy access to both the foyer and the gourmet kitchen. The breakfast room features a planning desk. Two family bedrooms share a bath to the left of the plan, while to the right a master suite enjoys a soaking tub, separate shower and walk-in closet.

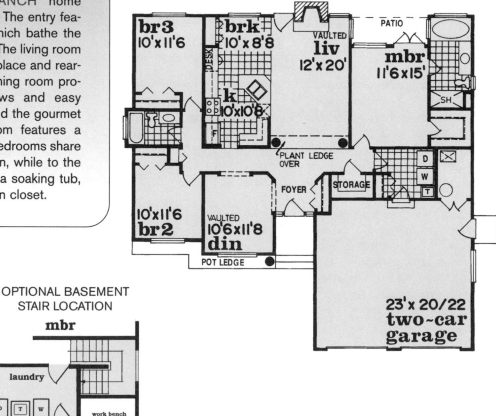

OPTIONAL BASEMENT
STAIR LOCATION

DESIGN
HPT890163

SQUARE FOOTAGE: 2,090
WIDTH: 67'-0" DEPTH: 59'-0"

THIS EXCITING SOUTHWESTERN design is enhanced by the use of arched windows and an inviting arched entrance. The large foyer opens to a massive great room with a fireplace and built-in cabinets. The kitchen features an island cooktop and a skylit breakfast area. The master suite has an impressive cathedral ceiling and a walk-in closet as well as a luxurious bath that boasts separate vanities, a corner whirlpool tub and a separate shower. Two additional bedrooms, which share a full bath, are located at the far end of the home for privacy.

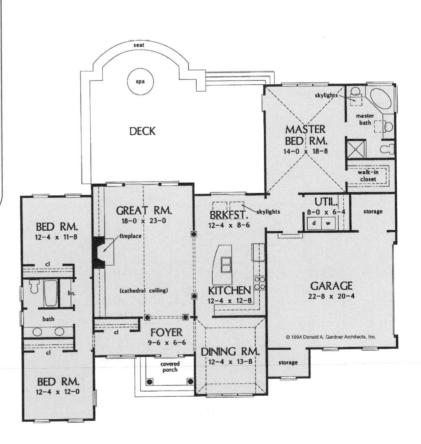

DESIGN
HPT890164

FIRST FLOOR: 1,463 SQ. FT.
SECOND FLOOR: 872 SQ. FT.
TOTAL: 2,335 SQ. FT.
WIDTH: 44'-0" DEPTH: 58'-10"

ARCHED WINDOWS AND STUCCO DETAILING combine to give this home plenty of charm. The interior plan begins with a vaulted foyer hosting a sweeping curved staircase spilling into a sunken living room with a masonry fireplace and vaulted ceiling. The kitchen has a pantry, center cooking island, built-in desk and sunny breakfast bay. A den with a walk-in closet and nearby bath can easily double as a guest room. The master suite on the second floor boasts a drop ceiling, bayed sitting area and lavish bath. The family bedrooms share a full bath.

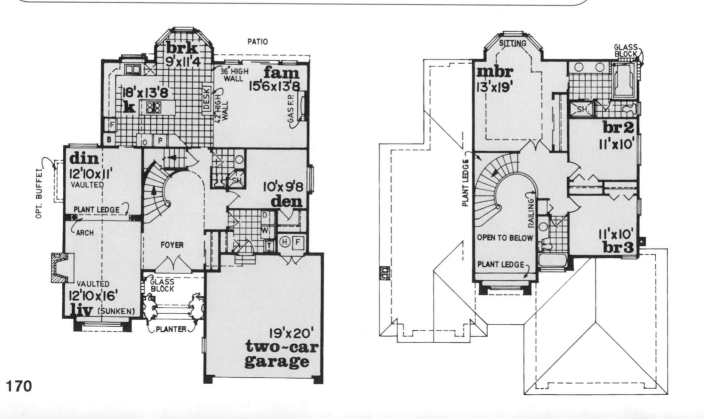

DESIGN
HPT890165

FIRST FLOOR: 1,230 SQ. FT.
SECOND FLOOR: 649 SQ. FT.
TOTAL: 1,879 SQ. FT.
WIDTH: 38'-0" DEPTH: 53'-6"

THE TILED FOYER of this two-story home opens to a living/dining space with a soaring ceiling, a fireplace in the living room and access to a covered patio that invites outdoor livability. The kitchen has an oversized, sunny breakfast area with a volume ceiling. The master bedroom offers privacy with its sumptuous bath; a corner soaking tub, dual lavatories and a compartmented toilet lend character to the room. Upstairs, a loft overlooking the living spaces could become a third bedroom. One of the family bedrooms features a walk-in closet. Both bedrooms share a generous hall bath.

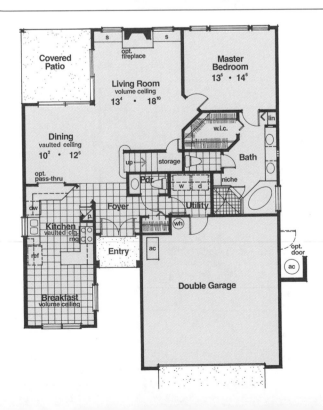

DESIGN
HPT890166

FIRST FLOOR: 1,776 SQ. FT.
SECOND FLOOR: 483 SQ. FT.
TOTAL: 2,259 SQ. FT.
WIDTH: 47'-0"   DEPTH: 64'-6"

TWO CIRCLE-TOP WINDOWS—one over the entry and one in the living room—echo the gentle arch over the recessed entry of this home. Double doors open to a center hall with a staircase to the second floor. The vaulted formal living and dining rooms are on the left. The sunken living room boasts a gas fireplace. The family room also has a vaulted ceiling and a gas fireplace and is brightened by skylights. In between sits the island kitchen with an attached breakfast bay. Sliding glass doors access a deck from the family room. The first-floor master suite holds a private deck, a through-fireplace to its well-appointed bath, and a walk-in closet. An additional bedroom with full bath and a den with private deck are found on the second floor.

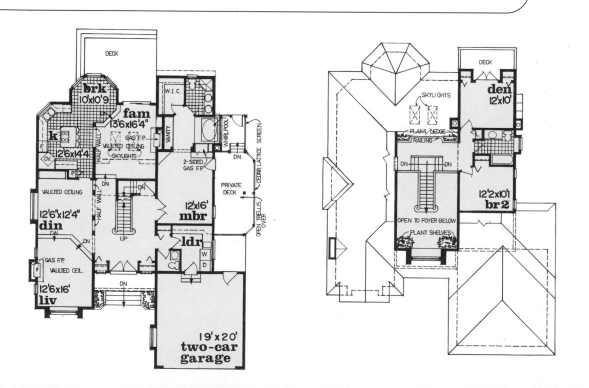

DESIGN
HPT890167

FIRST FLOOR: 1,195 SQ. FT.
SECOND FLOOR: 893 SQ. FT.
TOTAL: 2,088 SQ. FT.
WIDTH: 38'-0" DEPTH: 57'-8"

LOOKING FOR DRAMA AND SPACIOUSNESS? This design has volume rooflines to allow for vaulted ceilings in the living room, dining room and foyer. The gourmet kitchen, hearth-warmed family room and bumped-out breakfast nook form a large casual area for gatherings. Note the sliding glass doors in the family room leading to the rear yard. Positioned close to a full bath, the den can double easily as a guest room. Three second-floor bedrooms include a master suite, which features a private bath, vaulted ceiling and window seat. If you like, choose the three-car garage option.

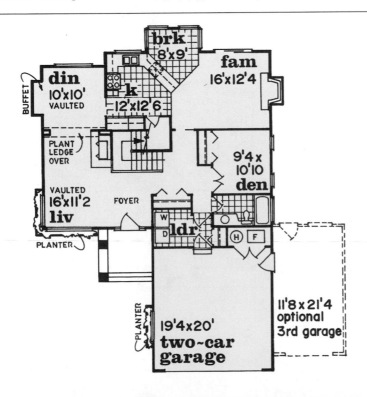

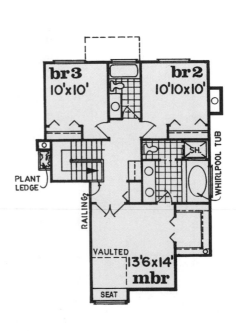

DESIGN
HPT890168

FIRST FLOOR: 1,520 SQ. FT.
SECOND FLOOR: 929 SQ. FT.
TOTAL: 2,449 SQ. FT.
WIDTH: 47'-0" DEPTH: 56'-6"

A RECESSED ENTRY WITH DOUBLE DOORS introduces this lovely plan. Vaulted ceilings throughout the foyer, living room, dining room and kitchen add a sense of spaciousness and allow for plant ledges. A peninsula fireplace separates the dining room and living room. The family room has another fireplace, flanked by shelves, to serve as an entertainment center. A private den sits adjacent to the family room. The master bedroom and the two family bedrooms reside on the upper level.

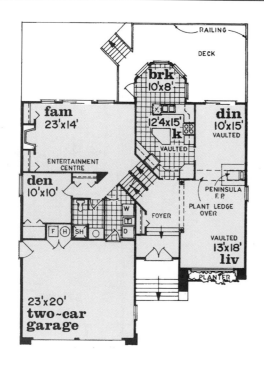

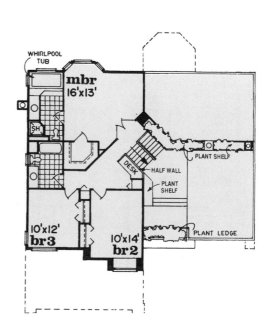

DESIGN
HPT890169

FIRST FLOOR: 2,121 SQ. FT.
SECOND FLOOR: 913 SQ. FT.
TOTAL: 3,034 SQ. FT.
WIDTH: 84'-0" DEPTH: 48'-0" **L D**

THIS STRIKING CONTEMPORARY design with Spanish good looks offers outstanding livability for today's active lifestyles. A three-car garage leads to a mudroom, laundry and washroom. An efficient, spacious kitchen opens to a large dining room, with a pass-through also leading to the family room. This room and the adjoining master bedroom suite overlook a backyard terrace. Just off the master bedroom is a sizable study that opens to a foyer. Stairs just off the foyer make upstairs access quick and easy. The hub of this terrific plan is a living room that faces the front courtyard, and a lounge above the living room. Upstairs, three family bedrooms share a bath and the spacious lounge.

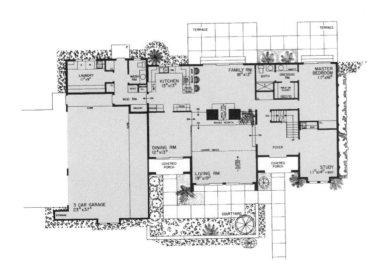

DESIGN
HPT890170

FIRST FLOOR: 1,731 SQ. FT.
SECOND FLOOR: 554 SQ. FT.
TOTAL: 2,285 SQ. FT.
WIDTH: 90'-2" DEPTH: 69'-10"

VARYING ROOF PLANES OF COLORFUL TILE surfaces help to make a dramatic statement. Privacy walls add appeal and help form the front courtyard and side private patio. The kitchen has an island cooktop, built-in ovens, a nearby walk-in pantry and direct access to the outdoor covered patio. The living room is impressive with its centered fireplace with long, raised hearth and access through French doors to the rear patio. At the opposite end of the plan is the master bedroom. It has a walk-in closet with shoe storage, twin lavatories in the bath, plus a whirlpool and stall shower. The two secondary bedrooms upstairs have direct access to a bath with twin lavatories. There is also a loft with open rail overlooking the curved stairway.

QUOTE ONE®

Cost to build? See page 182 to order complete cost estimate to build this house in your area!

DESIGN
HPT890171

FIRST FLOOR: 1,522 SQ. FT.
SECOND FLOOR: 800 SQ. FT.
TOTAL: 2,322 SQ. FT.
WIDTH: 69'-6" DEPTH: 56'-0" **L**

THIS TWO-STORY SPANISH MISSION-STYLE home has character inside and out. The first-floor master suite features a fireplace and gracious bath with a walk-in closet, a whirlpool, a shower, dual vanities and linen storage. A second fireplace serves both the gathering room and media room/library. The kitchen, with an island cooktop, includes a snack bar and an adjoining breakfast nook. Three bedrooms—one a wonderful guest suite—and two full baths occupy the second floor.

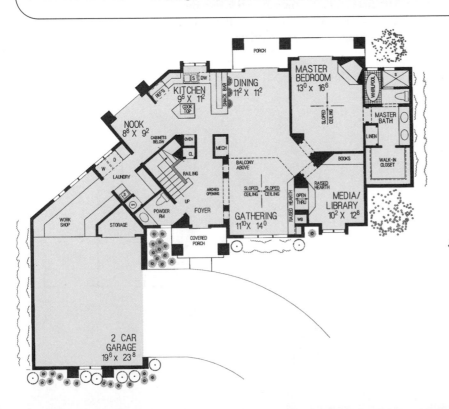

QUOTE ONE®

Cost to build? See page 182
to order complete cost estimate
to build this house in your area!

DESIGN
HPT890172

FIRST FLOOR: 1,911 SQ. FT.
SECOND FLOOR: 828 SQ. FT.
TOTAL: 2,739 SQ. FT.
WIDTH: 87'-10" DEPTH: 60'-8"

THE ARCHED COURTYARD ENTRANCE is a perfect introduction to this plan's wonderful livability—indoors and out. Open spaces and interesting angles greet you at the foyer, which is elegantly intersected with a curved stairway. The formal dining room opens to the large covered patio, perfect for entertaining and outdoor meals. The living room enjoys a dramatic corner fireplace with a raised hearth and is open to the oversized kitchen through a snack bar. A built-in breakfast booth joins the kitchen to the casual family room. The master suite is a welcome retreat thanks to a raised-hearth fireplace, patio door and lavish bath. Up the grand stairway, a lovely window bench frames the hallway leading to two family bedrooms, which share a compartmented bath, and to the guest suite with a private bath.

QUOTE ONE®
Cost to build? See page 182
to order complete cost estimate
to build this house in your area!

DESIGN
HPT890173

FIRST FLOOR: 1,966 SQ. FT.
SECOND FLOOR: 831 SQ. FT.
TOTAL: 2,797 SQ. FT.
WIDTH: 90'-0" DEPTH: 51'-8"

UNIQUE IN NATURE, this two-story Santa Fe-style home is as practical as it is lovely. The entry foyer leads past a curving staircase to living areas at the back of the plan. These include a living room with a corner fireplace and a family room connected to the kitchen via a built-in eating nook. The kitchen furthers its appeal with an island cooktop and a snack bar. Two family bedrooms on this level include one with a private covered patio. They share a full bath that includes dual lavatories and a whirlpool tub. Upstairs, the master suite features a grand bath, corner fireplace, large walk-in closet and private balcony. A guest bedroom accesses a full bath. Every room in this home has its own outdoor area.

Quote One®

Cost to build? See page 182
to order complete cost estimate
to build this house in your area!

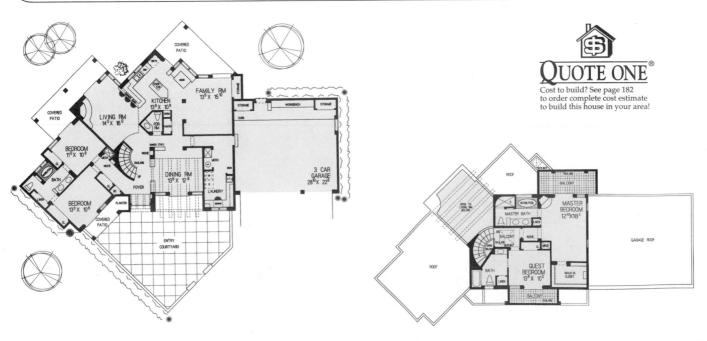

COPYRIGHT DOS & DON'TS

Blueprints for residential construction (or working drawings, as they are often called in the industry) are copyrighted intellectual property, protected under the terms of United States Copyright Law and, therefore, cannot be copied legally for use in building. However, we've made it easy for you to get what you need to build your home, without violating copyright law. Following are some guidelines to help you obtain the right number of copies for your chosen blueprint design.

COPYRIGHT DO

■ Do purchase enough copies of the blueprints to satisfy building requirements. As a rule for a home or project plan, you will need a set for yourself, two or three for your builder and subcontractors, two for the local building department, and one to three for your mortgage lender. You may want to check with your local building department or your builder to see how many they need before you purchase. You may need to buy eight to 10 sets; note that some areas of the country require purchase of vellums (also called reproducibles) instead of blueprints. Vellums can be written on and changed more easily than blueprints. Also, remember, plans are only good for one-time construction.

■ Do consider reverse blueprints if you want to flop the plan. Lettering and numbering will appear backward, but the reversed sets will help you and your builder better visualize the design.

■ Do take advantage of multiple-set discounts at the time you place your order. Usually, purchasing additional sets after you receive your initial order is not as cost-effective.

■ Do take advantage of vellums. Though they are a little more expensive, they can be changed, copied, and used for one-time construction of a home. You will receive a copyright release letter with your vellums that will allow you to have them copied.

■ Do talk with one of our professional service representatives before placing your order. They can give you great advice about what packages are available for your chosen design and what will work best for your particular situation.

COPYRIGHT DON'T

■ Don't think you should purchase only one set of blueprints for a building project. One is fine if you want to study the plan closely, but will not be enough for actual building.

■ Don't expect your builder or a copy center to make copies of standard blueprints. They cannot legally—most copy centers are aware of this.

■ Don't purchase standard blueprints if you know you'll want to make changes to the plans; vellums are a better value.

■ Don't use blueprints or vellums more than one time. Additional fees apply if you want to build more than one time from a set of drawings. ■

WHEN YOU'RE READY TO ORDER...

LET US SHOW YOU OUR HOME BLUEPRINT PACKAGE.

BUILDING A HOME? PLANNING A HOME?
OUR BLUEPRINT PACKAGE HAS NEARLY EVERYTHING YOU NEED TO GET THE JOB DONE RIGHT,

whether you're working on your own or with help from an architect, designer, builder or subcontractors. Each Blueprint Package is the result of many hours of work by licensed architects or professional designers.

QUALITY
Hundreds of hours of painstaking effort have gone into the development of your blueprint plan. Each home has been quality-checked by professionals to insure accuracy and buildability.

VALUE
Because we sell in volume, you can buy professional quality blueprints at a fraction of their development cost. With our plans, your dream home design costs substantially less than the fees charged by architects.

SERVICE
Once you've chosen your favorite home plan, you'll receive fast, efficient service whether you choose to mail or fax your order to us or call us toll free at 1-800-521-6797. After you have received your order, call for customer service toll free 1-888-690-1116.

SATISFACTION
Over 50 years of service to satisfied home plan buyers provide us unparalleled experience and knowledge in producing quality blueprints.

ORDER TOLL FREE 1-800-521-6797
After you've looked over our Blueprint Package and Important Extras, call toll free on our Blueprint Hotline: 1-800-521-6797, for current pricing and availability prior to mailing the order form on page 189. We're ready and eager to serve you. After you have received your order, call for customer service toll free 1-888-690-1116.

Each set of blueprints is an interrelated collection of detail sheets which includes components such as floor plans, interior and exterior elevations, dimensions, cross-sections, diagrams and notations. These sheets show exactly how your house is to be built.

SETS MAY INCLUDE:

FRONTAL SHEET
This artist's sketch of the exterior of the house gives you an idea of how the house will look when built and landscaped. Large floor plans show all levels of the house and provide an overview of your new home's livability, as well as a handy reference for deciding on furniture placement.

FOUNDATION PLANS
This sheet shows the foundation layout including support walls, excavated and unexcavated areas, if any, and foundation notes. If slab construction rather than basement, the plan shows footings and details for a monolithic slab. This page, or another in the set, may include a sample plot plan for locating your house on a building site.

DETAILED FLOOR PLANS
These plans show the layout of each floor of the house. Rooms and interior spaces are carefully dimensioned and keys are given for cross-section details provided later in the plans. The positions of electrical outlets and switches are shown.

HOUSE CROSS-SECTIONS
Large-scale views show sections or cut-aways of the foundation, interior walls, exterior walls, floors, stairways and roof details. Additional cross-sections may show important changes in floor, ceiling or roof heights or the relationship of one level to another. Extremely valuable for construction, these sections show exactly how the various parts of the house fit together.

INTERIOR ELEVATIONS
Many of our drawings show the design and placement of kitchen and bathroom cabinets, laundry areas, fireplaces, bookcases and other built-ins. Little "extras," such as mantelpiece and wainscoting drawings, plus molding sections, provide details that give your home that custom touch.

EXTERIOR ELEVATIONS
These drawings show the front, rear and sides of your house and give necessary notes on exterior materials and finishes. Particular attention is given to cornice detail, brick and stone accents or other finish items that make your home unique.

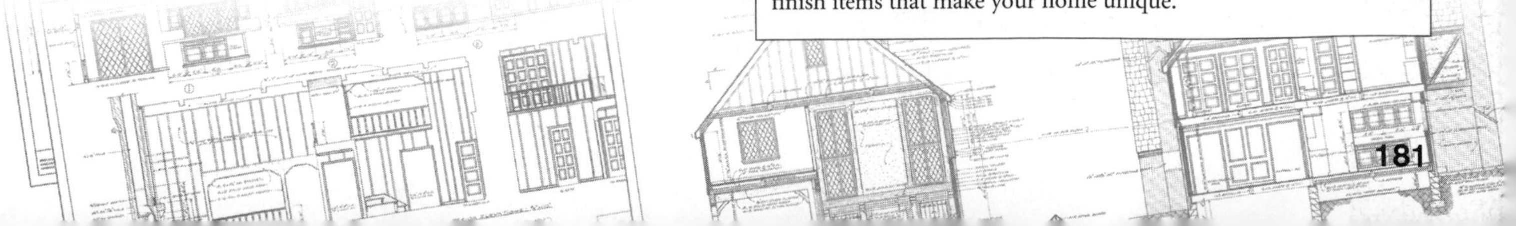

IMPORTANT EXTRAS TO DO THE JOB RIGHT!

INTRODUCING IMPORTANT PLANNING AND CONSTRUCTION AIDS DEVELOPED BY OUR PROFESSIONALS TO HELP YOU SUCCEED IN YOUR HOME-BUILDING PROJECT

MATERIALS LIST

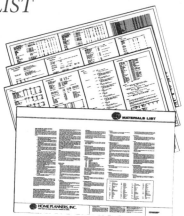

(Note: Because of the diversity of local building codes, our Materials List does not include mechanical materials.)

For many of the designs in our portfolio, we offer a customized materials take-off that is invaluable in planning and estimating the cost of your new home. This Materials List outlines the quantity, type and size of materials needed to build your house (with the exception of mechanical system items). Included are framing lumber, windows and doors, kitchen and bath cabinetry, rough and finish hardware, and much more. This handy list helps you or your builder cost out materials and serves as a reference sheet when you're compiling bids. Some Materials Lists may be ordered before blueprints are ordered, call for information.

SPECIFICATION OUTLINE

This valuable 16-page document is critical to building your house correctly. Designed to be filled in by you or your builder, this book lists 166 stages or items crucial to the building process. It provides a comprehensive review of the construction process and helps in choosing materials. When combined with the blueprints, a signed contract, and a schedule, it becomes a legal document and record for the building of your home.

QUOTE ONE®

SUMMARY COST REPORT   **MATERIAL COST REPORT**

A product for estimating the cost of building select designs, the Quote One® system is available in two separate stages: The Summary Cost Report and the Material Cost Report.

The **Summary Cost Report** is the first stage in the package and shows the total cost per square foot for your chosen home in your zip-code area and then breaks that cost down into various categories showing the costs for building materials, labor and installation. The report includes three grades: Budget, Standard and Custom. These reports allow you to evaluate your building budget and compare the costs of building a variety of homes in your area.

Make even more informed decisions about your home-building project with the second phase of our package, our **Material Cost Report.** This tool is invaluable in planning and estimating the cost of your new home. The material and installation (labor and equipment) cost is shown for each of over 1,000 line items provided in the Materials List (Standard grade), which is included when you purchase this estimating tool. It allows you to determine building costs for your specific zip-code area and for your chosen home design. Space is allowed for additional estimates from contractors and subcontractors, such as for mechanical materials, which are not included in our packages. This invaluable tool includes a Materials List. A Material Cost Report cannot be ordered before blueprints are ordered. Call for details. In addition, ask about our Home Planners Estimating Package.

If you are interested in a plan that is not indicated as Quote One®, please call and ask our sales reps. They will be happy to verify the status for you. To order these invaluable reports, use the order form.

CONSTRUCTION INFORMATION

If you want to know more about techniques—and deal more confidently with subcontractors — we offer these useful sheets. Each set is an excellent tool that will add to your understanding of these technical subjects. These helpful details provide general construction information and are not specific to any single plan.

PLUMBING

The Blueprint Package includes locations for all the plumbing fixtures, including sinks, lavatories, tubs, showers, toilets, laundry trays and water heaters. However, if you want to know more about the complete plumbing system, these Plumbing Details will prove very useful. Prepared to meet requirements of the National Plumbing Code, these fact-filled sheets give general information on pipe schedules, fittings, sump-pump details, water-softener hookups, septic system details and much more. Sheets also include a glossary of terms.

ELECTRICAL

The locations for every electrical switch, plug and outlet are shown in your Blueprint Package. However, these Electrical Details go further to take the mystery out of household electrical systems. Prepared to meet requirements of the National Electrical Code, these comprehensive drawings come packed with helpful information, including wire sizing, switch-installation schematics, cable-routing details, appliance wattage, doorbell hook-ups, typical service panel circuitry and much more. A glossary of terms is also included.

CONSTRUCTION

The Blueprint Package contains information an experienced builder needs to construct a particular house. However, it doesn't show all the ways that houses can be built, nor does it explain alternate construction methods. To help you understand how your house will be built—and offer additional techniques—this set of Construction Details depicts the materials and methods used to build foundations, fireplaces, walls, floors and roofs. Where appropriate, the drawings show acceptable alternatives.

MECHANICAL

These Mechanical Details contain fundamental principles and useful data that will help you make informed decisions and communicate with subcontractors about heating and cooling systems. Drawings contain instructions and samples that allow you to make simple load calculations, and preliminary sizing and costing analysis. Covered are the most commonly used systems from heat pumps to solar fuel systems. The package is filled with illustrations and diagrams to help you visualize components and how they relate to one another.

THE HANDS-ON HOME FURNITURE PLANNER

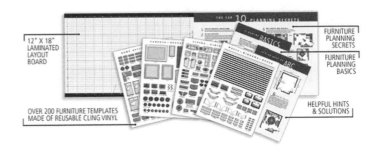

Effectively plan the space in your home using The **Hands-On Home Furniture Planner**. It's fun and easy—no more moving heavy pieces of furniture to see how the room will go together. And you can try different layouts, moving furniture at a whim.

The kit includes reusable peel and stick furniture templates that fit onto a 12" x 18" laminated layout board—space enough to layout every room in your home.

Also included in the package are a number of helpful planning tools. You'll receive:

- ✓ Helpful hints and solutions for difficult situations.
- ✓ Furniture planning basics to get you started.
- ✓ Furniture planning secrets that let you in on some of the tricks of professional designers.

The **Hands-On Home Furniture Planner** is the one tool that no new homeowner or home remodeler should be without. It's also a perfect housewarming gift!

To Order, Call Toll Free
1-800-521-6797

After you've looked over our Blueprint Package and Important Extras on these pages, call for current pricing and availability prior to mailing the order form. We're ready and eager to serve you. After you have received your order, call for customer service toll free 1-888-690-1116.

THE FINISHING TOUCHES...

THE DECK BLUEPRINT PACKAGE

Many of the homes in this book can be enhanced with a professionally designed Home Planners Deck Plan. Those homes marked with a **D** have a complementary Deck Plan, sold separately, which includes a Deck Plan Frontal Sheet, Deck Framing and Floor Plans, Deck Elevations and a Deck Materials List. A Standard Deck Details Package, also available, provides all the how-to information necessary for building *any* deck. Our Complete Deck Building Package contains one set of Custom Deck Plans of your choice, plus one set of Standard Deck Building Details, all for one low price. Our plans and details are carefully prepared in an easy-to-understand format that will guide you through every stage of your deck-building project. This page shows a sample Deck layout to match your favorite house. See Blueprint Price Schedule for ordering information.

THE LANDSCAPE BLUEPRINT PACKAGE

For the homes marked with an **L** in this book, Home Planners has created a front-yard Landscape Plan that is complementary in design to the house plan. These comprehensive blueprint packages include a Frontal Sheet, Plan View, Regionalized Plant & Materials List, a sheet on Planting and Maintaining Your Landscape, Zone Maps and Plant Size and Description Guide. These plans will help you achieve professional results, adding value and enjoyment to your property for years to come. Each set of blueprints is a full 18" x 24" in size with clear, complete instructions and easy-to-read type. A sample Landscape Plan is shown below. See Blueprint Price Schedule for ordering information.

CONTEMPORARY LEISURE DECK
Deck ODA021

CAPE COD COTTAGE
Landscape OLA003

REGIONAL ORDER MAP

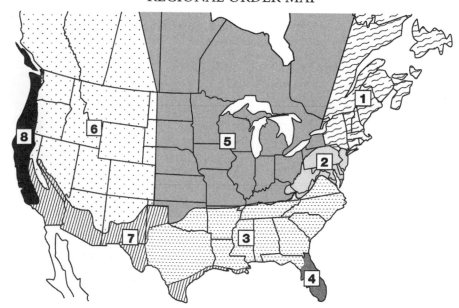

Most Landscape Plans are available with a Plant & Materials List adapted by horticultural experts to 8 different regions of the country. Please specify the Geographic Region when ordering your plan. See Blueprint Price Schedule for ordering information and regional availability.

Region	1	Northeast
Region	2	Mid-Atlantic
Region	3	Deep South
Region	4	Florida & Gulf Coast
Region	5	Midwest
Region	6	Rocky Mountains
Region	7	Southern California & Desert Southwest
Region	8	Northern California & Pacific Northwest

BLUEPRINT PRICE SCHEDULE

Prices guaranteed through December 31, 2003

TIERS	1-SET STUDY PACKAGE	4-SET BUILDING PACKAGE	8-SET BUILDING PACKAGE	1-SET REPRODUCIBLE*
P1	$20	$50	$90	$140
P2	$40	$70	$110	$160
P3	$70	$100	$140	$190
P4	$100	$130	$170	$220
P5	$140	$170	$210	$270
P6	$180	$210	$250	$310
A1	$440	$480	$520	$660
A2	$480	$520	$560	$720
A3	$530	$575	$615	$800
A4	$575	$620	$660	$870
C1	$620	$665	$710	$935
C2	$670	$715	$760	$1000
C3	$715	$760	$805	$1075
C4	$765	$810	$855	$1150
L1	$870	$925	$975	$1300
L2	$945	$1000	$1050	$1420
L3	$1050	$1105	$1155	$1575
L4	$1155	$1210	$1260	$1735
SQ1				.35/sq. ft.

* Requires a fax number

OPTIONS FOR PLANS IN TIERS A1–L4

Additional Identical Blueprints
in same order for "A1–L4" price plans ....$50 per set
Reverse Blueprints (mirror image)
with 4- or 8-set order for "A1–L4" plans.............................$50 fee per order
Specification Outlines...$10 each
Materials Lists for "A1–C3" plans ....$60 each
Materials Lists for "C4–L4" plans......................................$70 each

OPTIONS FOR PLANS IN TIERS P1–P6

Additional Identical Blueprints
in same order for "P1–P6" price plans...............................$10 per set
Reverse Blueprints (mirror image) for "P1–P6" price plans ....$10 fee per order
1 Set of Deck Construction Details ....$14.95 each
Deck Construction Package ....add $10 to Building Package price
*(includes 1 set of "P1–P6" plans, plus
1 set Standard Deck Construction Details)*

IMPORTANT NOTES
- SQ one-set building package includes one set of reproducible vellum construction drawings plus one set of study blueprints.
- The 1-set study package is marked "not for construction."
- Prices for 4- or 8-set Building Packages honored only at time of original order.
- Some foundations carry a $225 surcharge.
- Right-reading reverse blueprints, if available, will incur a $165 surcharge.
- Additional identical blueprints may be purchased within 60 days of original order.

To use the Index,

refer to the design number listed in numerical order (a helpful page reference is also given). Note the price tier and refer to the Blueprint Price Schedule above for the cost of one, four or eight sets of blueprints or the cost of a reproducible drawing. Additional prices are shown for identical and reverse blueprint sets, as well as a very useful Materials List for some of the plans. Also note in the Plan Index those plans that have Deck Plans or Landscape Plans. Refer to the schedules above for prices of these plans. The letter "Y" identifies plans that are part of our Quote One® estimating service and those that offer Materials Lists.

To order,

Call toll free 1-800-521-6797 for current pricing and availability prior to mailing the order form. FAX: 1-800-224-6699 or 520-544-3086.

PLAN INDEX

DESIGN	PRICE	PAGE	MATERIALS LIST	QUOTE ONE®	DECK	DECK PRICE	LANDSCAPE	LANDSCAPE PRICE	REGIONS
HPT890001	SQ1	4							
HPT890002	C1	6		Y			OLA014	P4	12345678
HPT890003	C3	8							
HPT890004	C3	10					OLA012	P3	12345678
HPT890005	C2	11							
HPT890006	C3	12							
HPT890007	C1	13	Y	Y					
HPT890008	C4	14					OLA004	P3	123568
HPT890009	A4	15							
HPT890010	A4	16							
HPT890011	A4	17					OLA024	P4	123568
HPT890012	C2	18	Y	Y			OLA024	P4	123568
HPT890013	C1	19					OLA001	P3	123568

PLAN INDEX

DESIGN	PRICE	PAGE	MATERIALS LIST	QUOTE ONE®	DECK	DECK PRICE	LANDSCAPE	LANDSCAPE PRICE	REGIONS
HPT890094	A2	100	Y						
HPT890095	C1	101							
HPT890096	C4	102							
HPT890097	C2	103							
HPT890098	A4	104	Y						
HPT890099	C2	105							
HPT890100	A1	106	Y						
HPT890101	A3	107							
HPT890102	A3	108							
HPT890103	A3	109	Y						
HPT890104	A2	110	Y						
HPT890105	A3	111	Y	Y					
HPT890106	A3	112	Y	Y					
HPT890107	C2	113							
HPT890108	A2	114	Y						
HPT890109	A2	115	Y						
HPT890110	A2	116							
HPT890111	C1	117							
HPT890112	A4	118	Y						
HPT890113	C1	119	Y	Y					
HPT890114	A3	120	Y						
HPT890115	A3	121	Y						
HPT890116	A3	122	Y						
HPT890117	A3	123							
HPT890118	A4	124							
HPT890119	A4	125	Y						
HPT890120	A3	126							
HPT890121	C1	127	Y						
HPT890122	A4	128	Y						
HPT890123	SQ1	129	Y						
HPT890124	C3	130	Y						
HPT890125	C4	131	Y						
HPT890126	C3	132	Y						
HPT890127	C2	133	Y						
HPT890128	C1	134	Y						
HPT890129	C1	135	Y	Y					
HPT890130	C1	136	Y	Y					
HPT890131	C1	137	Y						
HPT890132	A4	138	Y						
HPT890133	C2	139	Y	Y	ODA011	P2	OLA010	P3	1234568

PLAN INDEX

DESIGN	PRICE	PAGE	MATERIALS LIST	QUOTE ONE®	DECK	DECK PRICE	LANDSCAPE	LANDSCAPE PRICE	REGIONS
HPT890134	C2	140	Y						
HPT890135	C3	141							
HPT890136	C2	142							
HPT890137	C3	143							
HPT890138	A3	144	Y						
HPT890139	C1	145							
HPT890140	A4	146	Y		ODA011	P2	OLA083	P3	12345678
HPT890141	C2	147	Y	Y			OLA038	P3	7
HPT890142	A3	148	Y	Y					
HPT890143	C1	149	Y	Y			OLA033	P3	47
HPT890144	C3	150	Y						
HPT890145	C1	151	Y	Y			OLA038	P3	7
HPT890146	C1	152	Y	Y					
HPT890147	C3	153	Y						
HPT890148	C2	154	Y	Y			OLA034	P3	347
HPT890149	C2	155	Y	Y			OLA034	P3	347
HPT890150	C1	156	Y	Y			OLA038	P3	7
HPT890151	C1	157	Y						
HPT890152	C4	158	Y	Y			OLA037	P4	347
HPT890153	C3	159	Y	Y			OLA034	P3	347
HPT890154	C1	160	Y	Y			OLA040	P4	12345678
HPT890155	C2	161	Y				OLA037	P4	347
HPT890156	C1	162	Y	Y			OLA037	P4	347
HPT890157	C1	163							
HPT890158	A4	164							
HPT890159	C1	165							
HPT890160	A3	166							
HPT890161	C1	167							
HPT890162	A3	168	Y						
HPT890163	C1	169	Y						
HPT890164	A4	170	Y						
HPT890165	A4	171							
HPT890166	A4	172	Y						
HPT890167	A4	173	Y						
HPT890168	A4	174	Y						
HPT890169	C2	175	Y		ODA015	P2	OLA038	P3	7
HPT890170	A4	176	Y	Y					
HPT890171	A4	177	Y	Y			OLA013	P4	12345678
HPT890172	C1	178	Y	Y			OLA091	P3	12345678
HPT890173	C2	179	Y	Y			OLA034	P3	347

BEFORE FILLING OUT THE ORDER FORM, PLEASE CALL US ON OUR TOLL-FREE BLUEPRINT HOTLINE 1-800-521-6797. YOU MAY WANT TO LEARN MORE ABOUT OUR SERVICES AND PRODUCTS. HERE'S SOME INFORMATION YOU WILL FIND HELPFUL.

OUR EXCHANGE POLICY

With the exception of reproducible plan orders, we will exchange your entire first order for an equal or greater number of blueprints within our plan collection within 90 days of the original order. The entire content of your original order must be returned before an exchange will be processed. Please call our customer service department for your return authorization number and shipping instructions. If the returned blueprints look used, redlined or copied, we will not honor your exchange. Fees for exchanging your blueprints are as follows: 20% of the amount of the original order...plus the difference in cost if exchanging for a design in a higher price bracket or less the difference in cost if exchanging for a design in a lower price bracket. **(Reproducible blueprints are not exchangeable or refundable.)** Please call for current postage and handling prices. Shipping and handling charges are not refundable.

ABOUT REPRODUCIBLES

When purchasing a reproducible you may be required to furnish a fax number. The designer will fax documents that you must sign and return to them before shipping will take place.

ABOUT REVERSE BLUEPRINTS

Although lettering and dimensions will appear backward, reverses will be a useful aid if you decide to flop the plan. See Price Schedule and Plans Index for pricing.

REVISING, MODIFYING AND CUSTOMIZING PLANS

Like many homeowners who buy these plans, you and your builder, architect or engineer may want to make changes to them. We recommend purchase of a reproducible plan for any changes made by your builder, licensed architect or engineer. As set forth below, we cannot assume any responsibility for blueprints which have been changed, whether by you, your builder or by professionals selected by you or referred to you by us, because such individuals are outside our supervision and control.

ARCHITECTURAL AND ENGINEERING SEALS

Some cities and states are now requiring that a licensed architect or engineer review and "seal" a blueprint, or officially approve it, prior to construction due to concerns over energy costs, safety and other factors. Prior to application for a building permit or the start of actual construction, we strongly advise that you consult your local building official who can tell you if such a review is required.

ABOUT THE DESIGNS

The architects and designers whose work appears in this publication are among America's leading residential designers. Each plan was designed to meet the requirements of a nationally recognized model building code in effect at the time and place the plan was drawn. Because national building codes change from time to time, plans may not comply with any such code at the time they are sold to a customer. In addition, building officials may not accept these plans as final construction documents of record as the plans may need to be modified and additional drawings and details added to suit local conditions and requirements. We strongly advise that purchasers consult a licensed architect or engineer, and their local building official, before starting any construction related to these plans.

LOCAL BUILDING CODES AND ZONING REQUIREMENTS

At the time of creation, our plans are drawn to specifications published by the Building Officials and Code Administrators (BOCA) International, Inc.; the Southern Building Code Congress (SBCCI) International, Inc.; the International Conference of Building Officials (ICBO); or the Council of American Building Officials (CABO). Our plans are designed to meet or exceed national building standards. Because of the great differences in geography and climate throughout the United States and Canada, each state, county and municipality has its own building codes, zone requirements, ordinances and building regulations. Your plan may need to be modified to comply with local requirements regarding snow loads, energy codes, soil and seismic conditions and a wide range of other matters. In addition, you may need to obtain permits or inspections from local governments before and in the course of construction. Prior to using blueprints ordered from us, we strongly advise that you consult a licensed architect or engineer—and speak with your local building official—before applying for any permit or beginning construction. We authorize the use of our blueprints on the express condition that you strictly comply with all local building codes, zoning requirements and other applicable laws, regulations, ordinances and requirements. Notice: Plans for homes to be built in Nevada must be re-drawn by a Nevada-registered professional. Consult your building official for more information on this subject.

TOLL FREE 1-800-521-6797

REGULAR OFFICE HOURS:
8:00 a.m.-9:00 p.m. EST, Monday-Friday

If we receive your order by 3:00 p.m. EST, Monday-Friday, we'll process it and ship within **two business days**. When ordering by phone, please have your credit card or check information ready. We'll also ask you for the Order Form Key Number at the bottom of the order form.

By FAX: Copy the Order Form on the next page and send it on our FAX line: 1-800-224-6699 or 520-544-3086.

**Canadian Customers
Order Toll Free 1-877-223-6389**

ORDER FORM

DISCLAIMER

The designers we work with have put substantial care and effort into the creation of their blueprints. However, because they cannot provide on-site consultation, supervision and control over actual construction, and because of the great variance in local building requirements, building practices and soil, seismic, weather and other conditions, WE CANNOT MAKE ANY WARRANTY, EXPRESS OR IMPLIED, WITH RESPECT TO THE CONTENT OR USE OF THE BLUEPRINTS, INCLUDING BUT NOT LIMITED TO ANY WARRANTY OF MERCHANTABILITY OR OF FITNESS FOR A PARTICULAR PURPOSE. ITEMS, PRICES, TERMS AND CONDITIONS ARE SUBJECT TO CHANGE WITHOUT NOTICE. REPRODUCIBLE PLAN ORDERS MAY REQUIRE A CUSTOMER'S SIGNED RELEASE BEFORE SHIPPING.

TERMS AND CONDITIONS

These designs are protected under the terms of United States Copyright Law and may not be copied or reproduced in any way, by any means, unless you have purchased Reproducibles which clearly indicate your right to copy or reproduce. We authorize the use of your chosen design as an aid in the construction of one single family home only. You may not use this design to build a second or multiple dwellings without purchasing another blueprint or blueprints or paying additional design fees.

HOW MANY BLUEPRINTS DO YOU NEED?

Although a standard building package may satisfy many states, cities and counties, some plans may require certain changes. For your convenience, we have developed a Reproducible plan which allows a local professional to modify and make up to 10 copies of your revised plan. As our plans are all copyright protected, with your purchase of the Reproducible, we will supply you with a Copyright release letter. The number of copies you may need: 1 for owner; 3 for builder; 2 for local building department and 1-3 sets for your mortgage lender.

ORDER TOLL FREE!

For information about any of our services or to order call
1-800-521-6797

Browse our website:
www.eplans.com

BLUEPRINTS ARE NOT REFUNDABLE EXCHANGES ONLY

For Customer Service, call toll free
1-888-690-1116.

HOME PLANNERS, LLC wholly owned by Hanley-Wood, LLC
3275 WEST INA ROAD, SUITE 110 • TUCSON, ARIZONA • 85741

THE BASIC BLUEPRINT PACKAGE
Rush me the following (please refer to the Plans Index and Price Schedule in this section):
___Set(s) of reproducibles*, plan number(s) _____ $_____
    indicate foundation type _____ surcharge (if applicable): $_____
___Set(s) of blueprints, plan number(s) _____ indicate foundation type _____ $_____
    indicate foundation type _____ surcharge (if applicable): $_____
___Additional identical blueprints (standard or reverse) in same order @ $50 per set $_____
___Reverse blueprints @ $50 fee per order. Right-reading reverse @ $165 surcharge $_____

IMPORTANT EXTRAS
Rush me the following:
___Materials List: $60 (Must be purchased with Blueprint set.) Add $10 for Schedule C4–L4 plans $_____
___**Quote One®** Summary Cost Report @ $29.95 for one, $14.95 for each additional,
    for plans _____ $_____
    Building location: City _____ Zip Code _____
___**Quote One®** Material Cost Report @ $120 Schedules P1–C3; $130 Schedules C4–L4,
    for plan_____(Must be purchased with Blueprints set.) $_____
    Building location: City _____ Zip Code _____
___Specification Outlines @ $10 each $_____
___Detail Sets @ $14.95 each; any two $22.95; any three $29.95; all four for $39.95 (save $19.85) $_____
___❑ Plumbing ❑ Electrical ❑ Construction ❑ Mechanical
___Home Furniture Planner @ $15.95 each $_____

DECK BLUEPRINTS
(Please refer to the Plans Index and Price Schedule in this section)
___Set(s) of Deck Plan _____. $_____
___Additional identical blueprints in same order @ $10 per set. $_____
___Reverse blueprints @ $10 fee per order. $_____
___Set of Standard Deck Details @ $14.95 per set. $_____
___Set of Complete Deck Construction Package (Best Buy!) Add $10 to Building Package.
    Includes Custom Deck Plan _____ Plus Standard Deck Details

LANDSCAPE BLUEPRINTS
(Please refer to the Plans Index and Price Schedule in this section.)
___Set(s) of Landscape Plan _____ $_____
___Additional identical blueprints in same order @ $10 per set $_____
___Reverse blueprints @ $10 fee per order $_____
Please indicate appropriate region of the country for Plant & Material List. Region _____

POSTAGE AND HANDLING *SIGNATURE IS REQUIRED FOR ALL DELIVERIES.*	1–3 sets	4+ sets
DELIVERY No CODs (Requires street address—No P.O. Boxes)		
•Regular Service (Allow 7–10 business days delivery)	❑ $20.00	❑ $25.00
•Priority (Allow 4–5 business days delivery)	❑ $25.00	❑ $35.00
•Express (Allow 3 business days delivery)	❑ $35.00	❑ $45.00
OVERSEAS DELIVERY	fax, phone or mail for quote	

Note: All delivery times are from date Blueprint Package is shipped.

POSTAGE (From box above) $_____
SUBTOTAL $_____
SALES TAX (AZ & MI residents, please add appropriate state and local sales tax.) $_____
TOTAL (Subtotal and tax) $_____

YOUR ADDRESS (please print legibly)
Name _____
Street_____
City _____State_____Zip _____
Daytime telephone number (required) (_____) _____
* Fax number (required for reproducible orders) _____
TeleCheck® Checks By Phone℠ available
FOR CREDIT CARD ORDERS ONLY
Credit card number _____ Exp. Date: (M/Y) _____
Check one ❑ Visa ❑ MasterCard ❑ American Express

Order Form Key
HPT89

Signature (required) _____
Please check appropriate box: ❑ Licensed Builder-Contractor ❑ Homeowner

ORDER TOLL FREE!
1-800-521-6797

BY FAX: Copy the order form above and send it on
our FAXLINE: 1-800-224-6699 OR 520-544-3086

HELPFUL BOOKS FROM HOME PLANNERS

TO ORDER BY PHONE
1-800-322-6797

1 BIGGEST & BEST

1001 of our best-selling plans in one volume. 1,074 to 7,275 square feet. 704 pgs $12.95 1K1

2 ONE-STORY

450 designs for all lifestyles. 800 to 4,900 square feet. 384 pgs $9.95 OS

3 MORE ONE-STORY

475 superb one-level plans from 800 to 5,000 square feet. 448 pgs $9.95 MO2

4 TWO-STORY

443 designs for one-and-a-half and two stories. 1,500 to 6,000 square feet. 448 pgs $9.95 TS

5 VACATION

430 designs for recreation, retirement and leisure. 448 pgs $9.95 VS3

6 HILLSIDE

208 designs for split-levels, bi-levels, multi-levels and walkouts. 224 pgs $9.95 HH

7 FARMHOUSE

300 Fresh Designs from Classic to Modern. 320 pgs. $10.95 FCP

8 COUNTRY HOUSES

208 unique home plans that combine traditional style and modern livability. 224 pgs $9.95 CN

9 BUDGET-SMART

200 efficient plans from 7 top designers, that you can really afford to build! 224 pgs $8.95 BS

10 BARRIER-FREE

Over 1,700 products and 51 plans for accessible living. 128 pgs $15.95 UH

11 ENCYCLOPEDIA

500 exceptional plans for all styles and budgets—the best book of its kind! 528 pgs $9.95 ENC

12 ENCYCLOPEDIA II

500 completely new plans. Spacious and stylish designs for every budget and taste. 352 pgs $9.95 E2

13 AFFORDABLE

300 Modest plans for savvy homebuyers.256 pgs. $9.95 AH2

14 VICTORIAN

210 striking Victorian and Farmhouse designs from today's top designers. 224 pgs $15.95 VDH2

15 ESTATE

Dream big! Eighteen designers showcase their biggest and best plans. 224 pgs $16.95 EDH3

16 LUXURY

170 lavish designs, over 50% brand-new plans added to a most elegant collection. 192 pgs $12.95 LD3

17 EUROPEAN STYLES

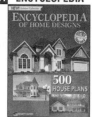

200 homes with a unique flair of the Old World. 224 pgs $15.95 EURO

18 COUNTRY CLASSICS

Donald Gardner's 101 best Country and Traditional home plans. 192 pgs $17.95 DAG

19 COUNTRY

85 Charming Designs from American Home Gallery. 160 pgs. $17.95 CTY

20 TRADITIONAL

85 timeless designs from the Design Traditions Library. 160 pgs. $17.95 TRA

21 COTTAGES

245 Delightful retreats from 825 to 3,500 square feet. 256 pgs. $10.95 COOL

22 CABINS TO VILLAS

Enchanting Homes for Mountain Sea or Sun, from the Sater collection. 144 pgs $19.95 CCV

23 CONTEMPORARY

The most complete and imaginative collection of contemporary designs available anywhere. 256 pgs. $10.95 CM2

24 FRENCH COUNTRY

Live every day in the French countryside using these plans, landscapes and interiors. 192 pgs. $14.95 PN

25 SOUTHERN

207 homes rich in Southern styling and comfort. 240 pgs $8.95 SH

26 SOUTHWESTERN

138 designs that capture the spirit of the Southwest. 144 pgs $10.95 SW

27 SHINGLE-STYLE

155 Home plans from Classic Colonials to Breezy Bungalows. 192 pgs. $12.95 SNG

28 NEIGHBORHOOD

170 designs with the feel of main street America. 192 pgs $12.95 TND

29 CRAFTSMAN

170 Home plans in the Craftsman and Bungalow style. 192 pgs $12.95 CC

30 GRAND VISTAS

200 Homes with a View. 224 pgs. $10.95 GV

190

Home Planners wants your building experience to be as pleasant and trouble-free as possible.
That's why we've expanded our library of do-it-yourself titles to help you along.

31 DUPLEX & TOWNHOMES

115 Duplex, Multiplex &
Townhome Designs. 128 pgs.
$17.95 MFH

32 WATERFRONT

200 designs perfect for your
waterside wonderland.
208 pgs $10.95 WF

33 NATURAL LIGHT

223 Sunny home plans for all
regions. 240 pgs. $8.95 NA

34 NOSTALGIA

100 Time-Honored designs
updated with today's features.
224 pgs. $14.95 NOS

35 STREET OF DREAMS

Over 300 photos showcase
54 prestigious homes.
256 pgs $19.95 SOD

36 NARROW-LOT

250 Designs for houses
17' to 50' wide. 256 pgs.
$9.95 NL2

37 SMALL HOUSES

Innovative plans for
sensible lifestyles.
224 pgs. $8.95 SM2

38 GARDENS & MORE

225 gardens, landscapes,
decks and more to
enhance every home.
320 pgs. $19.95 GLP

39 EASY-CARE

41 special landscapes
designed for beauty and
low maintenance.
160 pgs $14.95 ECL

40 BACKYARDS

40 designs focused solely on
creating your own specially
themed backyard oasis. 160
pgs $14.95 BYL

41 BEDS & BORDERS

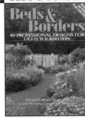

40 Professional designs
for do-it-yourselfers
160 pgs. $14.95 BB

42 BUYER'S GUIDE

A comprehensive look at 2700
products for all aspects of
landscaping & gardening.
128 pgs $19.95 LPBG

LANDSCAPE DESIGNS

43 OUTDOOR

74 easy-to-build designs,
lets you create and build
your own backyard oasis.
128 pgs $9.95 YG2

44 GARAGES

145 exciting projects from
64 to 1,900 square feet.
160 pgs. $9.95 GG2

45 DECKS

A brand new collection
of 120 beautiful and
practical decks. 144 pgs.
$9.95 DP2

46 HOME BUILDING

Everything you need to know
to work with contractors and
subcontractors. 212 pgs
$14.95 HBP

47 RURAL BUILDING

Everything you need to know
to build your home in the
country. 232 pgs.
$14.95 BYC

48 VACATION HOMES

Your complete guide to
building your vacation
home. 224 pgs.
$14.95 BYV

PROJECT GUIDES

Book Order Form

To order your books, just check the box of the book numbered below and complete the coupon. We will process
your order and ship it from our office within two business days. Send coupon and check (in U.S. funds).

YES! Please send me the books I've indicated:

❏ 1:1K1 ....$12.95	❏ 17:EURO ...$15.95	❏ 33:NA..........$8.95
❏ 2:OS...........$9.95	❏ 18:DAG $17.95	❏ 34:NOS $14.95
❏ 3:MO2........$9.95	❏ 19:CTY......$17.95	❏ 35:SOD $19.95
❏ 4:TS $9.95	❏ 20:TRA......$17.95	❏ 36:NL2........$9.95
❏ 5:VS3..........$9.95	❏ 21:COOL ..$10.95	❏ 37:SM2........$8.95
❏ 6:HH............$9.95	❏ 22:CCV......$19.95	❏ 38:GLP......$19.95
❏ 7:FCP........$10.95	❏ 23:CM2.....$10.95	❏ 39:ECL......$14.95
❏ 8:CN...........$9.95	❏ 24:PN........$14.95	❏ 40:BYL......$14.95
❏ 9:BS............$8.95	❏ 25:SH.........$8.95	❏ 41:BB........$14.95
❏ 10:UH $15.95	❏ 26:SW......$10.95	❏ 42:LPBG ..$19.95
❏ 11:ENC.......$9.95	❏ 27:SNG $12.95	❏ 43:YG2........$9.95
❏ 12:E2 ....$9.95	❏ 28:TND $12.95	❏ 44:GG2........$9.95
❏ 13:AH2........$9.95	❏ 29:CC $12.95	❏ 45:DP2........$9.95
❏ 14:VDH2 ...$15.95	❏ 30:GV.......$10.95	❏ 46:HBP $14.95
❏ 15:EDH3 ...$16.95	❏ 31:MFH....$17.95	❏ 47:BYC.....$14.95
❏ 16:LD3......$12.95	❏ 32:WF $10.95	❏ 48:BYV.....$14.95

Books Subtotal $_____
ADD Postage and Handling (allow 4–6 weeks for delivery) $ 4.00
Sales Tax: (AZ & MI residents, add state and local sales tax.) $_____
YOUR TOTAL (Subtotal, Postage/Handling, Tax) $_____

YOUR ADDRESS (PLEASE PRINT)

Name _____

Street _____

City _____ State _____ Zip _____

Phone (_____) _____ — _____

YOUR PAYMENT

TeleCheck® Checks By Phone℠ available

Check one: ❏ Check ❏ Visa ❏ MasterCard ❏ American Express

Required credit card information:

Credit Card Number _____

Expiration Date (Month/Year)_____ / _____

Signature Required _____

Home Planners, LLC
3275 W. Ina Road, Suite 110, Dept. BK, Tucson, AZ 85741

HPT89

Canadian Customers Order Toll Free 1-877-223-6389